NEWCOMER'S HANDBOOK®

Neighborhood GUiDE

Houston

2nd Edition

FIRST BOOKS®
PORTLAND • OREGON
WWW.FIRSTBOOKS.COM

© 2012 by Firstbooks.com, Inc. All rights reserved.

Newcomer's Handbook Neighborhood Guide for Houston

Newcomer's Handbook® and First Books® are registered trademarks of First Books.

Reproduction of the contents of this book in any form whatsoever is not permissible without written permission from the publishers, First Books®, 6750 SW Franklin Street, Suite A, Portland, OR 97223-2542, 503-968-6777., www.firstbooks.com.

First Books® is not legally responsible for any change in the value of any enterprises by reason of their inclusion or exclusion from this work. Contents are based on information believed to be accurate at the time of publication.

First Books® has not accepted payment from any firms or organizations for inclusion in this book.

Authors: Tracy Morris (2nd Edition); YuShan Chang (1st Edition)

Editor: Angela Brown
Series Editor: Linda Franklin
Publisher: Jeremy Solomon
Interior Layout and Composition: Emily Dueker, Masha Shubin
Maps: Jim Miller/fennana design
**Photographs by Tracy Morris
Cover photos: Open field (© JupiterImages), Houston Skyline (© Andy Z. BigStockPhoto.com), Mother & Daughter (© Cathleen Clapper. iStockPhoto.com), Rocket (© Kevin Tietz. BigStockPhoto.com), Theater District Statue (© Jim Domke. BigStockPhoto.com), Beach Riding (© Karin Lau. BigStockPhoto.com)

Paperback:
ISBN-13: 978-1-937090-41-8 | ISBN-10: 1-937090-41-8

ePub:
ISBN-13: 978-1-937090-42-5 | ISBN-10: 1-937090-42-6

Kindle:
ISBN-13: 978-1-937090-43-2 | ISBN-10: 1-937090-43-4

Printed in the U.S.A.
All paper is acid free and meets all ANSI standards for archival quality paper.

3 5 7 9 10 8 6 4 2

CONTENTS

- vii **INTRODUCTION**
- 1 **HOUSTON**
  - 2 **Inner Loop**
    - 3 Downtown, Midtown, and the Wards
      - 3 Downtown
- 4 **MAP: HOUSTON**
      - 7 Midtown
      - 8 The Wards
    - 10 Rice Military/Camp Logan/Crestwood/West End
    - 12 Heights
    - 14 East Houston
    - 18 Montrose
    - 19 Bellaire, West University Place, Southside Place, and Old Braeswood
    - 23 Museum/Medical Center
      - 23 Rice University Area/Museum District/Texas Medical Center
    - 25 Braeswood Place
    - 26 River Oaks/Upper Kirby/Greenway Plaza
      - 26 River Oaks
      - 27 Upper Kirby
      - 27 Greenway Plaza Area
  - 28 **Outer Loop**
    - 28 Uptown
    - 29 Tanglewood/Briargrove
    - 31 Westchase
    - 32 The Memorial Area
      - 33 The Villages

        34   Spring Valley
        35   Briar Forest
        35   Memorial West
        35   Spring Branch
   36   Katy and the Katy Area
   38   Addicks/Barker
39   **Southwest Houston**
   40   Meyerland
   41   Westbury
        42   Greater Fondren Southwest Area
        42   Glenshire
   44   Westwood/Harwin, Sharpstown, and Alief
        44   Westwood/Harwin
        44   Braeburn
        44   Sharpstown
        46   Alief
48   **Southwest Suburbs**
   48   Fort Bend County
   49   Meadows Place and Stafford
        49   Meadows Place
        49   Stafford
50   **MAP: GREATER HOUSTON**
   53   Sugar Land
   54   Missouri City
        55   Oyster Creek
        55   Lake Olympia
        55   Sienna Plantation
   57   Richmond and Rosenberg
58   **Northwest Houston**
   59   Inwood Forest, Candlelight, Garden Oaks, and Oak Forest
        59   Inwood Forest
        60   Candlelight
        60   Garden Oaks and Oak Forest
   61   Cypress Area
        61   Cypress
        62   Jersey Village
        62   Klein
        63   Champion Forest
        63   Gleannloch Farms
        64   Copperfield
        65   Fairfield
   66   Tomball
67   **North Houston and Surrounding Communities**
   67   Northline and Greenspoint

- 67 Northline
- 68 Greenspoint
- 69 Aldine and Spring
  - 69 Aldine
  - 69 Spring
- 71 Montgomery County
  - 71 The Woodlands
  - 72 Shenandoah

73 Northeast Houston
- 73 Humble
- 73 Kingwood
- 74 Atascocita

75 East of Houston
- 75 Pasadena, Deer Park, and Baytown
  - 75 Pasadena
  - 76 Deer Park
  - 77 Baytown
- 78 North Houston Ship Channel Area
- 80 La Porte Area

81 Bay Area
- 82 Clear Lake

84 Galveston County
- 85 Kemah
- 86 League City
- 87 Galveston
- 89 Texas City and La Marque
  - 89 Texas City
  - 89 La Marque

90 South of Houston
- 90 Brazoria County
  - 90 Brazosport Area
  - 91 Pearland
  - 92 Friendswood

95 INDEX

INTRODUCTION

THE SECOND LARGEST STATE IN THE US, TEXAS COVERS A DIVERSE GEOgraphic area of mountains, beaches, hills, piney woods, prairies, lakes, deserts, brush, rivers, valleys, and swamps. Texas' name is derived from the Caddo Indian tribe word "tejas," which means "friend." Indeed, the state motto is friendship, which is reflected in the amiable character of its residents.

Six flags have flown over the state of Texas (French, Spanish, Mexican, Texas, Confederate, and American), resulting in the blending of Spanish, Mexican, French, Southern, American, and frontier West cultures that have shaped the traditions and culture of Texas. Early French explorers established an unsuccessful post, Fort St. Louis, which was eventually taken over by the Spanish, who claimed Texas as a colony of Spain, known as New Spain. After Mexico's independence from Spain in 1821, Texas became the northern section of the Coahuila y Tejas state of Mexico. Unsatisfied with Mexican rule, the "Texians" fought for independence from Mexico in a war that lasted from October 1835 to April 1836, ending at the Battle of San Jacinto. The war at sea, however, continued well into the 1840s, with Mexico refusing to acknowledge Texas independence and the US largely refusing funds on the basis of budget constraints.

Finally, in 1848, Mexico recognized Texas' independence with the signing of the Treaty of Guadalupe Hidalgo.

For nine years after San Jacinto, the Republic of Texas remained an independent country until it was admitted into the Union as the 28th state in 1845. The state, however, seceded from the Union during the Civil War and joined the Confederate States of America. It was readmitted into the Union in 1870.

Texas is also known as the Lone Star State because of the single star on the Texas state flag. It is the second most populous state in the Union. Six Texas cities are in the top 25 most populous cities in the US (Houston, San Antonio, Dallas, Fort Worth, Austin, and El Paso). Because of its size, Texas covers part of the American

South and part of the American Southwest. The state shares characteristics of both of these regions, but different cities may be more heavily influenced by one region, depending on its location. The state is in the Central Time Zone, except for the far western tip where El Paso is located, which is in the Mountain Time Zone.

Though there has been a growing interest in living inside the city, the majority of residents in the state's major cities live in suburbs, which are the fastest growing areas of the state. This can largely be attributed to the price of housing and quality of the school districts in the suburbs. Many of the new suburban communities are major developments in once rural, unincorporated areas outside of municipalities. Suburbs in unincorporated areas receive their utilities through municipal utility districts ("MUD"), governmental entities specially formed to provide utilities to residents. MUDs are funded by a MUD tax, one of several other taxes that are levied on a homestead or make up a homeowner's property tax. Other taxes on homes may include those levied by counties, school districts, cities, college districts, and hospital districts. The largest tax on a homeowner's property is typically the school district tax, which may be anywhere from $1,500 to well over $10,000 a year, depending on the value of the property. Therefore, while the property may be a bargain, buyers should research the annual school district and property tax on a home before purchasing.

Increasing population, road congestion, and environmental concerns have prompted many Texas cities to construct light rail lines and plan for other forms of public transportation. The most widely used form of transportation, however, is still the personal vehicle. As a result, multi-lane freeways are part of the landscape of every major Texas city. As suburban sprawl causes cities to expand farther outward, rural roads known as FM (farm to market) and RM (ranch to market) have been incorporated into the new communities as local roads and freeways.

Freeways in metropolitan areas of Texas can be very confusing to non-locals. In Houston, three major roads and highways encircle the city. The beltways, starting from inside the city, are Loop 610, Beltway 8/Sam Houston Tollway, and the partially completed Grand Parkway, which, when completed, will become the world's largest "loop." One of the most common problems newcomers will encounter is the multiple names for one freeway. As in many areas of the country, stretches of freeways in major Texas cities are commonly referred to by their local name, which often pertains to a geographical location or was renamed in honor of a famous civic or political leader. This may confuse newcomers who are unaccustomed to the local freeway names, so below is a guide to navigating the area's major metropolitan freeways.

HOUSTON

US 59 South	south of downtown to Sugarland	Southwest Freeway
US 59 North	north of downtown to Kingwood	Eastex Freeway
I-10 West	west of downtown to Katy	Katy Freeway
I-10 East	east of downtown to Baytown	East Freeway
I-45 South	south of downtown to Galveston	Gulf Freeway
I-45 North	north of downtown to Conroe	North Freeway
US 290 North	north of Memorial to Cypress	Northwest Freeway
State Highway (S.H.) 288	south of downtown to Pearland	South Freeway
Loop 610		The Loop
State Highway 99		Grand Parkway

HOUSTON

"**H**OUSTON, WE HAVE A PROBLEM." EVER SINCE APOLLO 13 ASTROnaut James Lovell first uttered that memorable phrase, the city has been associated with NASA and entered the nation's consciousness as Space City, one of the city's nicknames. Houston, however, is more popularly known as the Bayou City because of its many bayous (slow-moving waterways along low-lying or swampy land) that cross through it. In 1836, brothers Augustus and John Allen founded Houston on the banks of Buffalo Bayou. The two enterprising businessmen had dreams of turning their plot of real estate along the navigable bayous into a successful commercial town. They named the town in honor of General Sam Houston, the hero of the Battle of San Jacinto during the fight for Texas' independence from Mexico and the Republic's first president. Since those early beginnings as a small commerce and frontier town, Houston has transformed itself into a diverse, cosmopolitan city and grown into the nation's sixth most populous metropolitan area.

Unlike most major US cities, Houston has no zoning laws, which has resulted in several urban districts instead of a single city center. The unofficial districts in Houston are Medical Center, Theater District, NASA area, Galleria/Uptown, Memorial/River Oaks, Museum District, Downtown, Midtown, Southwest, Northside/airport, Northwest/Cypress, and Eastside. This decentralized layout has contributed to the city's sprawl. Drive an hour in any direction and you'll likely still be in Houston. Freeways and the personal vehicles play a major role in Houstonians' lives. At times traffic can be difficult, especially with the seemingly endless road construction and expansion, but residents usually handle these challenges with patience and grace. It's customary for one driver to let another into traffic, which is appreciated with a hand wave. One surefire way to identify yourself as a nonresident is to honk your horn during a traffic jam.

Several industries besides the US manned space flight program are major players in the relatively stable Houston economy. These include the world's largest medical center, 40 percent of the nation's capacity for chemical production, agribusiness, computer software and electronics, nanotechnology, and financial/insurance/real estate services. Still, the city is primarily impacted by the energy industry. While New York has the financial district, Los Angeles the motion picture industry, and Detroit automobile manufacturing, Houston is known worldwide as a key oil, gas, and energy center. Since the famed Spindletop derrick gushed forth oil 90 miles away in Beaumont in 1901, Houston has been at the forefront of oil-related technology, refining, and distribution. The Port of Houston is a key factor in the city's position as a major energy market. Houston is home to more than 3600 energy-related companies, including the headquarters of 17 Fortune 500 companies and 600 exploration and production firms. Many of these companies are foreign firms that represent countries from every continent. This has contributed to sizable expatriate communities in addition to the several immigrant communities in Houston. Significant international populations include Vietnamese, Chinese, South Asian, Nigerian/African, South American, Mexican, Central American, British, Middle Eastern, and a smaller group of European expatriates composed primarily of French, Germans, Dutch, and Belgians.

Houston is a city of immigrants and migrants with an optimistic attitude. The city has 94 foreign consulates. From the oil boom of the 1970s, when approximately 1,300 people a week, mostly from the Rust Belt states, were moving into the city, to the rush of more than 200,000 New Orleanians fleeing Hurricane Katrina in 2005, Houston consistently has attracted people seeking to make a fortune or a fresh start. The cost of living here is relatively low, housing is affordable, and the semi-tropical climate makes the city green year 'round. These are just a few of the reasons why each year thousands of new residents call Houston their home.

INNER LOOP

The Inner Loop is the area inside Interstate 610, one of the several major freeways that circle Houston. Revitalization initiatives have made it a much sought-after residential area. In addition to four universities, two medical schools, and one of the largest community colleges in the country, many of Houston's visitor attractions are inside the Loop, including downtown, the Theater District, Main Street bars and restaurants, the Toyota Center for basketball and hockey, Minute Maid (baseball) Park, Houston Dynamo soccer stadium, the Museum District, the Houston Zoo, Hermann and Memorial Parks, the Texas Medical Center, and the George R. Brown Convention Center. Living "inside the Loop" has long been a desirable location and lifestyle. Communities inside Loop 610 include Montrose, River Oaks, Bellaire, West University/Southside Place, Upper Kirby, Museum District, Rice Military/Camp Logan/Crestwood, downtown, Midtown, Heights, the six historic wards, East End/Harrisburg, and the Rice University area.

DOWNTOWN, MIDTOWN, AND THE WARDS
Downtown

Boundaries: North: I-10 (Katy Freeway); **East:** Chartres; **South:** US 59 (Southwest Freeway); **West:** Bagby

Downtown is Houston's Central Business District. It has undergone an amazing transformation in the last 20 years. Originally, the area was strictly a business and commercial area with imposing steel, glass, and concrete structures. With the exception of the **Theater District**, where the symphony, ballet, music, theater, and opera venues are located, there were few reasons other than work for residents to come downtown since most of the more casual entertainment and sports venues were located in other parts of the city.

These days, there are plenty of reasons to come, play, and live in downtown Houston. Aggressive revitalization of the area has supported the opening of new residences, shops, restaurants, hotels, and bars. The formerly all-business appearance of Main Street, in particular, has been enlivened by the inclusion of local designers' input, which has resulted in a pedestrian-friendly cosmopolitan atmosphere. Smart tile and glass artwork decorates the light rail platforms; sidewalks are dotted with sculpture fountains and trees; and people-watching while dining al fresco is a weekend favorite.

Loft living has boomed in downtown Houston as developers, in an about-face from the city's future-focused tendencies, have found real estate treasures in the many older buildings formerly used as warehouses. Several of the buildings encourage a small community atmosphere by hosting social events for the young professionals and empty nesters who fill the majority of these ultra-modernized residences, which are for sale and lease.

Downtown

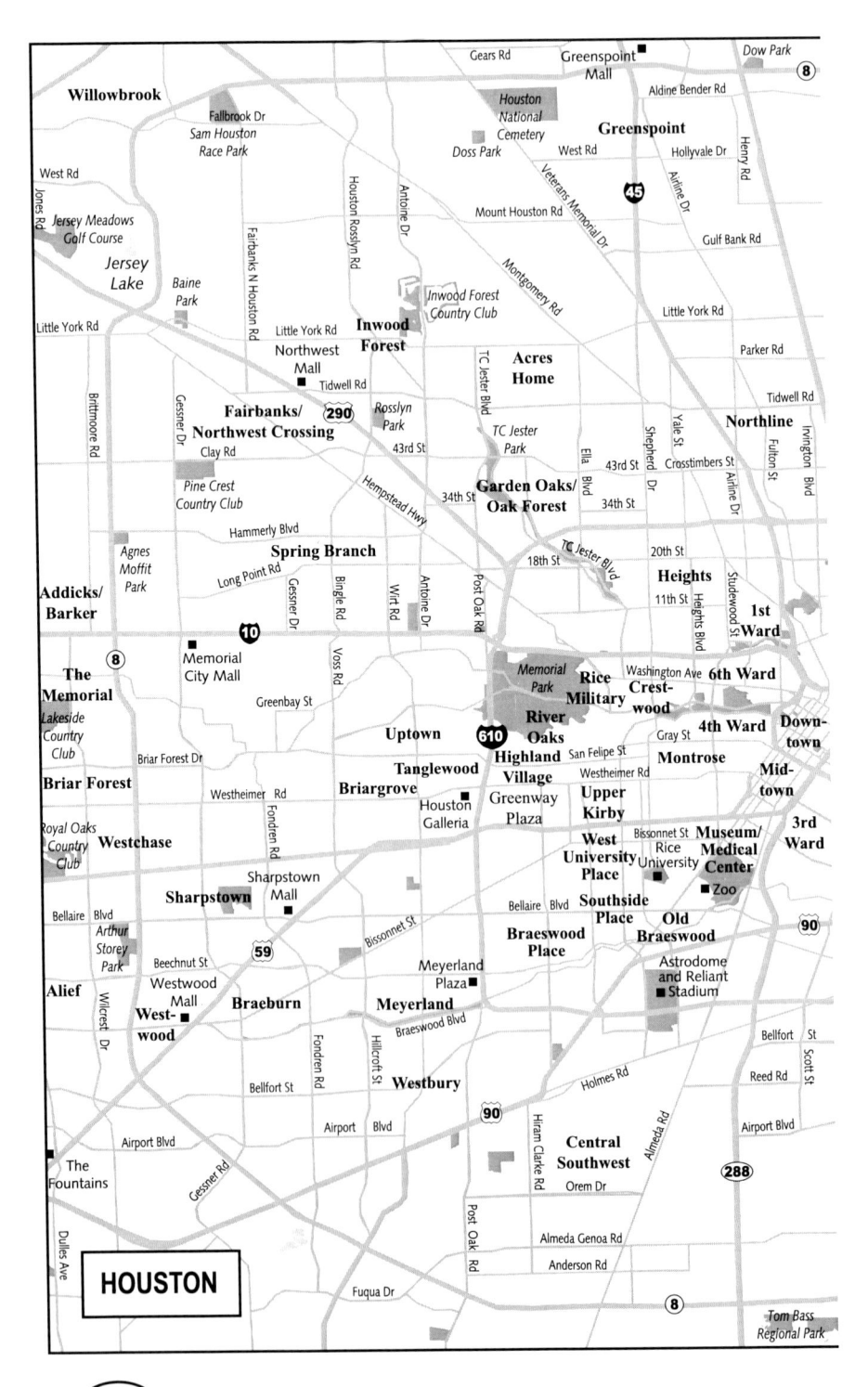

HOUSTON

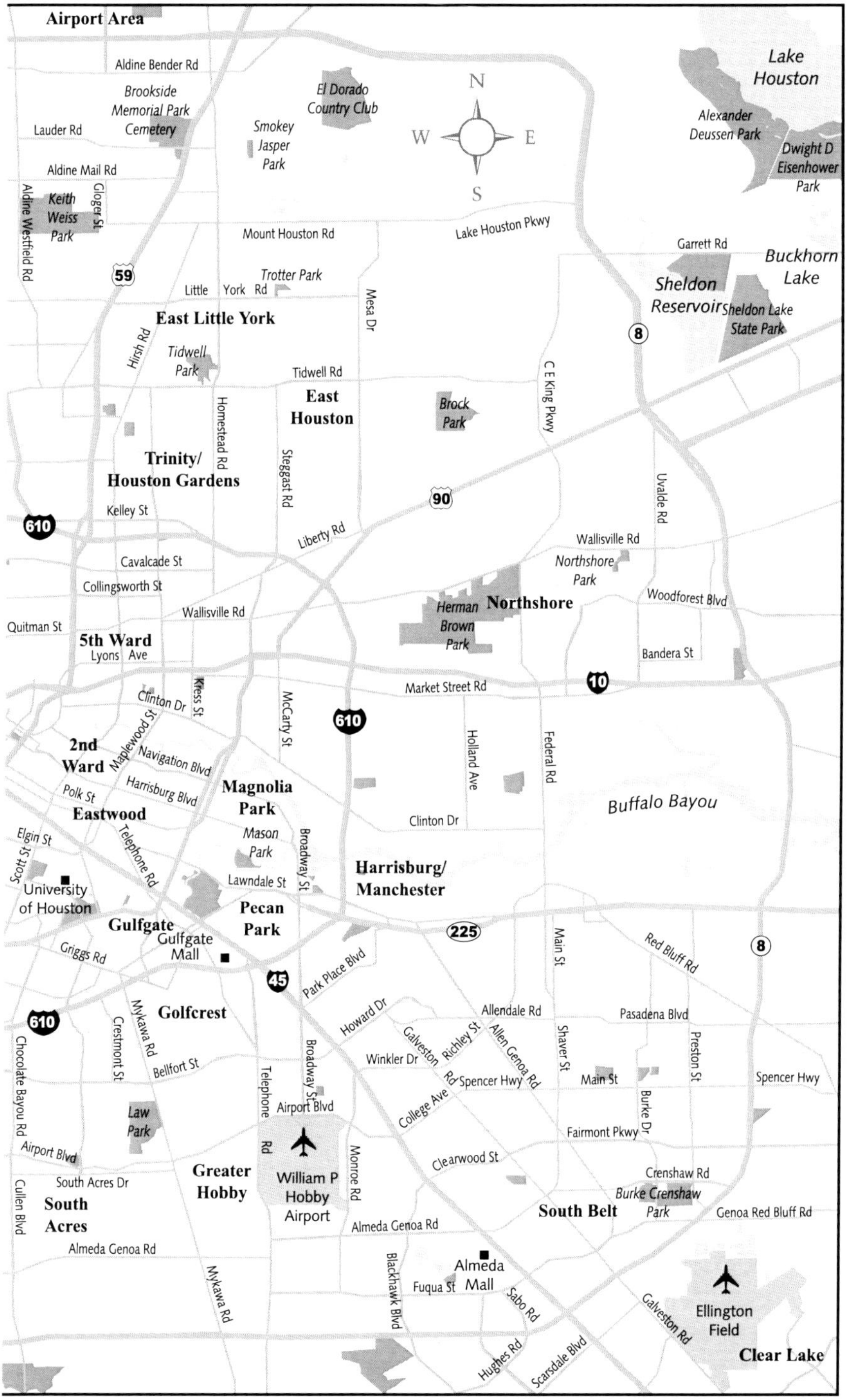
Airport Area
Aldine Bender Rd
Brookside Memorial Park Cemetery
Lauder Rd
Aldine Mail Rd
Aldine Westfield Rd
Keith Weiss Park
Gloger St
El Dorado Country Club
Smokey Jasper Park
N
W
E
S
Lake Houston
Alexander Deussen Park
Dwight D Eisenhower Park
Mount Houston Rd
Lake Houston Pkwy
Garrett Rd
Buckhorn Lake
Sheldon Reservoir
Sheldon Lake State Park
59
Little York Rd
Trotter Park
East Little York
Mesa Dr
8
Hirsh Rd
Tidwell Park
Tidwell Rd
East Houston
Brock Park
C E King Pkwy
Homestead Rd
Steggast Rd
Trinity/ Houston Gardens
Uvalde Rd
90
Kelley St
610
Liberty Rd
Wallisville Rd
Northshore Park
Cavalcade St
Collingsworth St
Woodforest Blvd
Wallisville Rd
Herman Brown Park
Northshore
Quitman St
5th Ward
Lyons Ave
Bandera St
Kress St
Clinton Dr
McCarty St
Market Street Rd
10
610
2nd Ward
Maplewood St
Navigation Blvd
Holland Ave
Federal Rd
Harrisburg Blvd
Polk St
Magnolia Park
Buffalo Bayou
Eastwood
Clinton Dr
Elgin St
Telephone Rd
Mason Park
Broadway St
Scott St
Harrisburg/ Manchester
Lawndale St
University of Houston
Pecan Park
Gulfgate
Gulfgate Mall
225
Main St
Red Bluff Rd
8
Griggs Rd
Park Place Blvd
45
610
Golfcrest
Howard Dr
Allendale Rd
Pasadena Blvd
Chocolate Bayou Rd
Crestmont St
Mykawa Rd
Galveston Rd
Richley St
Allen Genoa Rd
Shaver St
Preston St
Bellfort St
Winkler Dr
Spencer Hwy
Main St
Spencer Hwy
Broadway St
Telephone Rd
Airport Blvd
College Ave
Burke Dr
Law Park
Fairmont Pkwy
Airport Blvd
Clearwood St
Greater Hobby
William P Hobby Airport
Monroe Rd
Crenshaw Rd
South Acres Dr
Burke Crenshaw Park
South Acres
Cullen Blvd
South Belt
Genoa Red Bluff Rd
Almeda Genoa Rd
Almeda Genoa Rd
Blackhawk Blvd
Almeda Mall
Fuqua St
Mykawa Rd
Sabo Rd
Galveston Rd
Ellington Field
Clear Lake
Hughes Rd
Scarsdale Blvd

Despite economic hard times around the country in the first decade of the 2000s, Houston's relatively stable economy has allowed investment and speculation in downtown real estate and development. Minute Maid Park, which hosted the 2004 MLB All-Star Game, and the Toyota Center, host to the 2006 NBA All-Star Game, are now bookends to Houston's latest recreation and business area, bounded by an elevated portion of Interstate 59 and LaBranch Street. Between the two stadiums, the George R. Brown Convention Center is busy hosting large indoor gatherings, while just outside, Discovery Green, Houston's newest urban green space, offers a range of relaxation opportunities from casual dining to live music to outdoor movies, yoga, dance classes, and much more. On the other side of downtown in the Theater District, historical venues, including Jones Hall, the Alley Theatre, and the Wortham Center, are now joined by Houston Ballet's brand-new Center for Dance and the Bayou Place entertainment complex, which features restaurants, the Verizon Wireless Theater concert venue, and residential lofts. Jones Plaza, a public outdoor square across the street, hosts concerts, social gatherings, and outdoor viewing parties during the World Series playoffs and other major sporting events. The Hobby Center's Zilkha and Sarofim Halls bring both large-scale and intimate theater and musical performances, in addition to fine dining and commissioned art exhibits, to Houston's venerated 17-block Theater District, one of the largest in the US, second in number of seats only to New York City. One of the most ambitious downtown projects has been the revitalization of a 10-mile stretch of Buffalo Bayou, considered the birthplace of Houston. Terraced riverwalks, landings, parks, and hike/bike trails extend from Memorial Park eastward through downtown to the city's historical East End.

Houston is famous for its forward thinking and focus on the future, but historic structures remain in downtown surrounded by newer gleaming towers. Examples of Houston's recent reverence for its history include Market Square, the Renaissance Revival–style old Cotton Exchange, The Italianate Esperson Building, art deco–style City Hall, turn-of-the-century brick Julia Ideson branch of the Houston Public Library, and the former Rice Hotel—now luxury loft residences—where JFK slept before that fateful afternoon in Dallas.

For more near-downtown living, look to **Allen Parkway** at the northern border of the Montrose area. New apartments, luxury condos, and townhomes in all varieties of architectural designs and colors line the southern side of winding, scenic Allen Parkway, which leads straight into downtown from Shepherd Drive. No matter how hot or humid the weather, joggers can be seen daily along the Buffalo Bayou's sculpture-dotted greenbelt that lines the thoroughfare, and Eleanor Tinsley Park is the spot for city-wide music festivals and fireworks displays. Folk art lovers around the world know Allen Parkway as the annual scene of the world's first and largest art car parade.

Midtown

Boundaries: North: I-45; **East:** SH 288; **South:** US 59; **West:** Fourth Ward & Montrose

One of the earliest residential communities after the city's founding by the Allen brothers, Midtown, originally known as Southside Place, was home to prosperous families of the Humble Oil & Refinery Company's founders. The area fell into decline during the oil bust of the 1980s, which affected the city's housing market. The community of Victorian-style homes dating back to the turn of the century in this area that flourished in post–World War II decades was nearly abandoned by the 1990s. Then, a hot housing market and a demand for housing inside the city led to the development and revitalization of this area with its own Midtown Redevelopment Authority. Midtown is a primarily residential urban section ideally situated between the city's two biggest employment areas, Downtown and the Texas Medical Center, and near several of Houston's major universities. Apartments, townhomes, and lofts have replaced almost all of the aging wooden homes. Only a handful of these homes remain, and many are being restored to their former elegant state.

Midtown is home to Houston's original Vietnamese business district, formally designated as Little Saigon by the city in 2004. While the area's revitalization resulted in property tax increases that saw many Little Saigon businesses move west, Vietnamese street signs posted around several Midtown blocks still denote the influential presence of this ethnic commercial district. Midtown's rebirth has paved the way for Houston's urban residential revival with new mixed-use, pedestrian-friendly developments (a rarity in car-dependent Houston) that feature brick sidewalks, outdoor patios, shops on the ground floors of lofts, pubs, and restaurants. With the opening of grocery stores, drugstores, strip shopping centers, and other amenities across from residential complexes, Midtown slowly has become a viable residential community again. With wonderful views of the downtown

Midtown

skyline at night, Midtown lounges, bars, and clubs are among the most popular nightspots in Houston. On weekends, the streets are lined with cars and young urban professionals.

The Wards

A historic designation of six areas that straddle or are part of various neighborhoods, including downtown (Third Ward), Midtown (Fourth Ward), and East Houston (Second Ward).

In the shadow of downtown's skyscrapers lies a cluster of historic communities with origins in old political subdivisions known as wards. Though political wards were abolished in the early 1900s, the areas here continue to be known as the First, Second, Third, Fourth, Fifth, and Sixth Wards. The wards have a reputation as low-income minority neighborhoods. Though this is true to some degree, not all the property values here are depressed nor are they all undesirable areas in which to live. In fact, some of the wards and areas around them are experiencing heavy investment and revitalization that have people clamoring to move there. Other wards have lovely established neighborhoods, unknown even to many Houstonians, which go for above-average property prices.

First Ward is located north of Congress Avenue and west of Main Street, immediately northwest of downtown, next to the Theater District. It was the city's first business district, originally included the Woodland Heights portion of the Houston Heights neighborhood, and is today home to many of Houston's oldest buildings. Currently an ethnically diverse neighborhood composed of Hispanic, African-American, and white residents, First Ward was in the 1900s a working class community inhabited mainly by African-Americans and Italian immigrants. University of Houston's downtown campus is here as well as the landmark Old Jeff Davis Hospital, which originally served as the city's first public hospital and was later used for a variety of purposes including a sanitarium and warehouse. Abandoned for many years, this historic neoclassical building was restored and has been converted into affordable loft apartments for artists.

Second Ward is roughly bounded by Buffalo Bayou to the north, Lockwood Avenue to the east, railroad tracks to the south, and Congress Street to the west. Originally an upper-class suburb at the beginning of the 20th century, it still features many of its original large homes standing next to smaller, more recently constructed homes. Most of the buildings here were built in the 1920s and feature the art deco style. The area experienced white flight after World War II, and today it is a predominantly Hispanic neighborhood. There are many industrial buildings here, especially on the northern end along Buffalo Bayou. New development has begun in the past few years, with loft apartments constructed on the western boundary. Some of the buildings on the west side near Minute Maid Park have been converted into lofts.

The historic African-American neighborhood of **Third Ward** was settled by freed slaves at the end of the Civil War. Project Row House, a public art project that features 22 restored shotgun houses (narrow, rectangular, one-story dwellings with no halls), is located here. Another notable site in Third Ward is Emancipation Park, built in the late 1800s. Texas Southern University, a historically black college, and the University of Houston are both located in Third Ward. For information on residential areas surrounding the universities, refer to the **East Houston** section.

Fourth Ward is known as Freedman's Town because it was founded by freed slaves. This historic community is becoming an endangered community because of the gentrification of neighboring Midtown and downtown. Many of the shotgun-style houses that line the brick paved streets are in poor condition. This is an unfortunate period in the history of a community that at the height of its glory was considered this city's Harlem, with jazz clubs and restaurants.

Fifth Ward is north of Buffalo Bayou and east of Little Oak Bayou. Founded after the Civil War by freed slaves, Fifth Ward is one of the city's oldest black neighborhoods. During the 1920s many black people from Louisiana migrated here and opened up businesses. Their influence can be seen in some of the architecture in this neighborhood. At one time, Fifth Ward was a major industrial and transportation center.

Sixth Ward is below First Ward and bounded by Washington, Houston, and Capitol streets and the Glenwood Cemetery. It is listed on the National Register of Historic Places for its large collection of intact wood-frame Victorian homes. Though many of these homes are in shabby condition, preservation efforts have begun and are continuing. The two major streets here are Washington Avenue and Memorial Drive.

Websites: www.houstonmidtown.com, www.downtownhouston.org, www.houstontheaterdistrict.org, www.houstontx.gov
Area Code: 713

Sixth Ward

Zip Codes: 77002, 77010

Post Offices: Sam Houston Finance Station, 701 San Jacinto St, Ste 149; Civic Center Station, 700 Smith St; Sam Houston Carrier Station, 1500 Hadley St; Houston Station, 401 Franklin St

Police Precincts: Houston Police Department: Central Division, 61 Riesner St, 713-247-4400; Downtown Patrol, 1415 Fannin St, Ste 200, 713-308-8000

Emergency Hospitals: St. Joseph Medical Center, www.sjmctx.com, 1401 St. Joseph Pkwy, 713-757-1000; Texas Medical Center, www.tmc.edu: Hermann Hospital, www.memorialhermann.org, 6411 Fannin St, 713-704-4000; Ben Taub, www.hchdonline.com, Ben Taub General Hospital, 1504 Taub Loop, 713-873-2000; Methodist Hospital, www.methodisthealth.com, 6565 Fannin St, 713-790-3311; VA Hospital, www.houston.va.gov, 2002 Holcombe Blvd, 800-553-2278; St. Luke's, www.sleh.com, 6720 Bertner Ave, 832-355-1000; Texas Children's Hospital, www.texaschildrenshospital.org, 6621 Fannin St, 832-824-1000

Adult Education: Houston Community College–Central Campus, http://ccollege.hccs.edu, 1300 Holman St, 713-718-6000; University of Houston Downtown, www.uhd.edu, One Main St, 713-221-8000; South Texas College of Law, www.stcl.edu, 1303 San Jacinto St, 77002, 713-659-8040

Public Education: Houston Independent School District, www.houstonisd.org, 4400 W 18th St, 713-556-6005

Community Publications: *Houston Chronicle*, www.chron.com; *Houston Press*, www.houstonpress.com

Community Resources: City Hall, 900 Bagby St, 713-837-0311; YMCA Downtown, www.ymcahouston.org, 1600 Louisiana St, 713-659-8501

Public Transportation: Metropolitan Transit Authority of Harris County, www.ridemetro.org: Metro Light Rail; *Bus:* Midtown: 1, 8, 11, 60, 65, 132, 163, 261, 262, 265, 274, 283, 292, 297; Downtown: 1, 5, 8, 15, 25, 52, 78, 44, 56, 79, 20, 102, 108, 201, 202, 204, 212, 283, 131, 214, 216, 221, 228, 48, 50, 37, 40, 77, 30, 6, 3, 70, 36, 40, 60, 30, 80, 77, 88, 11, 15, 35, 52, 60, 163, 261, 262, 265, 274, 35, 53, 82, 283, 9

RICE MILITARY/CAMP LOGAN/CRESTWOOD/WEST END

Located along the winding streets next to scenic Memorial Park and across from the Memorial neighborhood, Rice Military and Camp Logan are two popular residential neighborhoods. Although the area once had been largely forgotten and somewhat neglected, people are rediscovering the beauty and tranquility of the Rice Military and Camp Logan subdivisions. Much of the appeal lies in their location inside 610 Loop, near downtown, the Medical Center, and the Galleria area. This has not gone unnoticed by developers, who have descended into the area in the past few years to build new homes, including many townhomes. This upper-middle-class neighborhood is now one of the hottest residential markets in Houston.

Many neighborhoods and communities are located near the city center and its amenities, but few have **Rice Military**'s advantage of immediately bordering **Memorial Park**. This scenic oasis, Houston's answer to Central Park, is one of the city's most cherished public areas. It was named Memorial Park in commemoration of the lives lost during World War I. During World War I, it was the site of a US Army training camp known as Camp Logan, the namesake of the present-day neighborhood. One of the most notable chapters in Houston and US history occurred in 1917, when soldiers from the camp were involved in a racially charged riot that resulted in a citywide curfew and the court martial of more than 100 men. The park's land was donated in 1924 by William C. Hogg, a wealthy influential turn-of-the-century city leader. Covering 1,466 square miles, Memorial Park has one of the best urban biking, hiking, and jogging trails. In addition, it features a soccer field, a highly rated municipal golf course, horse rentals, and other amenities. Like the area in general, towering pine trees and large leafy trees cover the park, creating a forest in the heart of the city. It attracts not only nearby residents but citizens from across the city who are attracted by the excellent running and walking trails and golf course. The trails are open 24 hours and lighted at night. This popular park is often crowded, and it is often difficult to get a spot on the golf course.

Houston's latest hot spot, the Washington Corridor runs along the northern edge of the Rice Military area. One of the locale's original thoroughfares for farmers who carted their produce from western farms to market in the center of Houston, Washington Avenue was until recently in relative decay. Now it's lined with eateries, clubs, and music venues in every range of expense. It's even become the city's hub of the latest food craze, the mobile food scene, or "food truck dining." Partiers here can choose to park in the many pay-parking lots and stroll Washington Avenue, or hire the city's first official jitney service in years, The Wave, to shuttle them up and down the avenue.

The neighborhood along the Washington Corridor is referred to simply as the **West End**. Many original homes are still here, and gentrification is in full swing. So you'll find a mix of remodeled modern along with rundown abandoned buildings and transformed warehouses. The location appeals to lovers of urban art, nightlife, and old dwellings. Part of the West End recently has been named Houston's Arts District.

Rice Military contains a mix of single-story and two-story homes of unique designs that range from $300,000 to more than $750,000. In addition, many new three- and four-story high-end townhomes recently have been constructed in **Camp Logan**, replacing the tiny bungalows in Rice Military. Like the park next to it, these subdivisions are surrounded by tall trees and lush, lavishly landscaped lawns. The origins of Rice Military's name are unclear. It appears, however, to have been named after the family of Rice University founder William Marsh Rice, whose relatives once owned most of the area. This subdivision predates Camp Logan, so "military" was most likely added when Rice Institute, now Rice University, was converted to a military school–like environment during World War I.

Crestwood, just east of Memorial Park, features spacious, new custom homes on large lots that range from $500,000 to more than $2 million. The original neighborhood was built in the 1930s, and nearly all of the original residences have been demolished.

Websites: www.houstontx.gov, www.ricemilitary.org
Area Code: 713
Zip Code: 77007
Post Offices: Heights Station, 1050 Yale St; River Oaks Station, 1900 W Gray St
Police Precinct: Houston Police Department: Central Division, 61 Riesner St, 713-247-4400
Emergency Hospitals: Memorial Hermann Hospital–Memorial City, www.memorialhermann.org, 921 Gessner Rd; Texas Medical Center, www.tmc.edu: Hermann Hospital, www.memorialhermann.org, 6411 Fannin St, 713-704-4000; Ben Taub, www.hchdonline.com, Ben Taub General Hospital, 1504 Taub Loop, 713-873-2000; Methodist Hospital, www.methodisthealth.com, 6565 Fannin St, 713-790-3311; VA Hospital, www.houston.med.va.gov, 2002 Holcombe Blvd, 1-800-553-2278; St. Luke's, www.sleh.com, 6720 Bertner Ave, 832-355-1000; Texas Children's Hospital, www.texaschildrenshospital.org, 6621 Fannin St, 832-824-1000
Library: Houston Public Library, Looscan Branch, 2510 Willowick Rd
Public Education: Houston Independent School District, www.houstonisd.org, 4400 W 18th St, 713-556-6005
Community Publications: *Houston Chronicle*, www.chron.com; *Houston Press*, www.houstonpress.com
Community Resources: City Hall, 900 Bagby St, 713-837-0311; Memorial Park, 6501 Memorial Dr, 713-845-1000
Public Transportation: Metropolitan Transit Authority of Harris County, www.ridemetro.org: *Bus:* 6, 20, 36, 70, 85; The Wave, www.thehoustonwave.com

HEIGHTS

Boundaries: North: Loop 610; **East:** Yale and Oxford; **South:** I-10; **West:** Dian and Blare

Although Houston has been particularly bad about preserving its historic buildings, the historic Heights area is an exception, best known for its well preserved and restored Craftsman homes and Victorian mansions. A small-town community located within the heart of the city, the Heights even has its own opera company and newspaper. Some neighborhood businesses are well known, established shops that have been operated by the same family for generations. The best time to shop in the Heights is the first Saturday of each month, when retailers offer specials and in-store activities.

HOUSTON: INNER LOOP

Heights

Established in 1896 as a small town outside of Houston, the community was named for its location on relatively higher land (62 feet above sea level) above White Oak Bayou. In fact, it is the highest point in the city. At the time of its annexation by the City of Houston in 1918, it had a population of approximately 9,000. During the 1950s the Heights began to decline but was revitalized in the 1970s by residents interested in preserving its history and architecture. Today several of the buildings are listed on the National Register of Historic Places, and the neighborhood is noted by a Texas Historical Commission marker. Though the Heights is currently a livable and desirable neighborhood, approximately 30 years ago it was a high-crime area. Some shady areas still border this community, but as redevelopment expands throughout the Heights and neighboring areas, the criminal elements and disreputable character of some areas may slowly disappear as they have with past redevelopment projects.

The Heights area includes the pricy, tree-filled **Woodland Heights** neighborhood and the less expensive **Sunset Heights**, whose small bungalows and farm houses from a distant era are under siege from townhouse builders. Woodland Heights features mostly historic bungalows with wide verandas and overhanging eaves, as well as cottages, foursquares, and Victorian mansions. Another section of the Heights, called **Norhill**, has tidy, smaller homes on lots with fewer trees. A nearby neighborhood with historic homes with similar architectural designs is **Timbergrove West** to the west.

Websites: www.houstonheights.org, www.woodland-heights.org, www.houstontx.gov
Area Code: 713
Zip Code: 77008
Post Offices: TW House Station, 1300 W 19th St; Heights Station, 1050 Yale St; Anson Jones Station, 634 W Cavalcade St

NEIGHBORHOOD GUIDE: HOUSTON

Police Precincts: Houston Police Department: Heights Storefront, 910 N Durham, # D, 713-803-1151; Central Division, 61 Riesner St, 713-247-4400
Emergency Hospital: St. Joseph's Hospital, www.sjmctx.com, 1401 St. Joseph Pkwy, 713-757-1000
Library: Houston Public Library, www.hpl.lib.tx.us: Heights Branch, 1302 Heights Blvd, 832-393-1810
Public Education: Houston Independent School District, www.houstonisd.org, 4400 W 18th St, 713-556-6005
Community Publications: *Houston Tribune,* www.houstontribune.com; *Heights Pages,* www.heightspages.com; *Houston Chronicle,* www.chron.com; *Houston Press,* www.houstonpress.com
Community Resources: Greater Heights Chamber of Commerce, www.heightschamber.com, 545 W 19th St, 713-861-6735; HITS Unicorn Theater, www.hitstheatre.org, 311 W 18th St, 713-861-7408
Public Transportation: Harris County Metropolitan Transit Authority, www.ridemetro.org. *Bus:* 8, 9, 26, 27, 34, 40, 50

EAST HOUSTON

Boundaries: North: I-10; **East:** 610; **South:** I-45; **West:** US 59

Houston's origin and past lie in the East End, with many of the city's early settlements and industries located here. The city's urban factories and industrial plants, including the Oak Farms Dairy plant, oil refineries, Maximus Coffee Group, Sara Lee Bakery Group, and Anheuser-Busch brewery, are concentrated in East Houston. The biggest economic engine here, however, is the Port of Houston, the nation's number one port for foreign cargo.

East Houston

In the early part of the 20th century, East Houston was a melting pot of German, Italian, and Latino families. Today it contains two of Houston's oldest Hispanic neighborhoods, **Magnolia Park** and **Second Ward**. The murals, artwork, Catholic churches, and neighborhood institutions attest to the area's cultural identity. Established neighborhood stores, restaurants, and mercados create a unique atmosphere and proud ethnic character in these mostly working-class Hispanic communities. While it is true that the east end of Houston is a center of Latino culture, this section of Houston has a diverse population where other cultures coexist. The largest portion of the East End is situated just east of I-45, across from two major universities, the University of Houston and Texas Southern University, as well as Houston Community College. The Orange Show, a well-known folk art center and springboard of the country's oldest and largest art car parade, is also located here. In recent decades this area has attracted the interests of developers, which may change the character of the community, but for now the East End is still mostly influenced by the families who have called it home for many decades.

East Houston has somewhat of a negative albeit over-generalized reputation because of parts of the area's heavy industrialization and accompanying pollution, pockets of largely low-income residents, and supposed crime rate. Parts of it can be an eyesore and it lacks some of the amenities, luxuries, and glamour of other parts of Houston, but it still is a relatively safe and diverse community. There are several charming neighborhoods with historic homes and nice lawns. East Houston is essentially the inner city with many local mom-and-pop shops and independently owned businesses. Do not expect to find any big box stores, chain restaurants, or malls in the area. In some areas supermarkets tend to be smaller, and in some cases the nearest food store is a small neighborhood grocery shop. Neighborhoods in Houston's East End include the following:

Lindale Park, north of I-10, east of the Heights, contains bungalows from the 1950s set among large trees. This is one of those lovely established neighborhoods with character and charm.

Idylwood is bounded by Lawndale Street on the north, Brays Bayou on the east, Sylvan Road on the south, and Wayside Drive on the west. Cottage-style bungalows here are reminiscent of the style and architecture of highly desirable neighborhoods such as the Heights or West University but much more affordable. This charming and beautiful neighborhood sits on a small hill that slopes down into Buffalo Bayou while tall pines and oaks line the winding streets. On the west, a large, wooded area surrounding the Villa de Matel Catholic convent borders the neighborhood known as **Country Club Place**, where civic club signs proudly announce it was established in 1941. Nearby are other hidden East Houston finds such as **Mason Park, Pecan Park,** and **Glen Brook**.

Though people generally do not consider the area surrounding the **University of Houston/Texas Southern University** as a place to live because of its perceived crime rate and lack of nearby amenities, there are many neighborhoods hidden behind the campuses that are as lovely and charming as those in more desirable areas such as West University or the Heights. They feature grand historic homes, smaller graceful residences, and lovely lawns. These neighborhoods have character and charm that are often lacking in the newer, suburban developments. They include **Washington Terrace** to the west of Texas Southern University and bounded by Almeda to the west, Alabama to the north, and Blodgett to the south. This has historically been and still is a neighborhood where the city's affluent African-American citizens reside. South of the University of Houston is **University Oaks,** once home to many faculty of this large, public institution that has recently been named as a Tier One Research University.

Farther south from Blodgett, between North and South MacGregor, is **Riverside Terrace**. In the segregated 1930s, Riverside Terrace was the location for well-to-do Jewish families who were not allowed to build in posh River Oaks. Many of Houston's more famous founding families were from Riverside. Over time, the Civil Rights Movement brought change, first in the form of violence, then demographic change. Riverside Terrace transformed into the prime location for African-American professionals to live. Its proximity to two universities meant many professors made their home among the stately mansions built on oversize, thickly wooded lots. Now Riverside Terrace is a mix of revitalization and still-neglected properties.

One of the oldest communities in Houston has recently experienced revitalization as more people seek affordable residences inside the Loop. During its heyday, **Eastwood** was a master-planned community where notable Houstonians such as billionaire Howard Hughes grew up. Later characterized by graffiti, abandoned buildings, and blight, it is once again a lovely neighborhood aesthetically on par with some of Houston's most esteemed residential areas. Single professionals, couples, and young families have restored many of the historic Craftsman and Prairie-style homes. The charm and architecture of this neighborhood is reminiscent of the Heights but more affordable. In fact, it is a good option for those desiring to live in a close-knit neighborhood with the grace, history, and character of the Heights but without the price tag. People who are priced out of the Montrose or Heights neighborhoods often opt for Eastwood. Located near downtown Houston, Eastwood offers residents the advantage of being near the city's major sports venues, Theater District, and nightlife.

At present, two additional rail lines are being built in the near-end east side of Houston—one that runs from Downtown east along Harrisburg Boulevard to the Magnolia area, and another from Downtown east and south through the UH-TSU complex and MacGregor Park area and ending at Palm Center.

The status of the **Gulfgate** neighborhood is best reflected in the fortunes of Gulfgate Mall, the city's first indoor regional shopping mall. Once an upscale shopping destination, it fell into decline during the late 1960s and early 1970s as other malls opened alongside new residential developments in the suburbs. It was a time of flight to the suburbs, and the average household income dropped significantly. Since then, the average income here has remained at around the same level. Today, Gulfgate is a predominantly Hispanic community where many recent immigrants reside. Its location along the intersection of Loop 610 and I-45, however, attracts a diverse population to the businesses by the freeways.

An initiative by the city and private developers intended to revive the community's economy recently culminated in the million-dollar redevelopment of Gulfgate Mall and shopping center. Nevertheless, it is unlikely that Gulfgate will return to the middle-class neighborhood of yesteryear. The community is not targeted for urban gentrification, which would bring higher income residents into the area. In addition, the Hispanic new immigrant community has established deep roots and strong connections that have cemented their presence and influence in Gulfgate.

Other nearby neighborhoods include **Harrisburg** (which was once a town all its own and the Allen brothers' first choice of locations to build Houston), **Manchester, Golfcrest,** and **Magnolia Park.**

Websites: www.houstontx.gov, www.greatereastend.com, www.idylwood.org, www.lindalepark.org

Area Code: 713

Zip Codes: 77003, 77004, 77011, 77020, 77087

Post Offices: Franklin Station, 401 Franklin St; Sam Houston Finance Station, 701 San Jacinto St, Ste 149; Sam Houston Carrier Station, 1500 Hadley St; Southmore Station, 4110 Almeda Rd; Jensen Drive Station, 3520 Jensen Dr; Broadway Station, 4020 Broadway St

Police Precincts: Houston Police Department: Central Patrol, 61 Riesner St, 713-247-4400; East Patrol (Magnolia), 7425 Sherman St, 713-928-4600; Lyons Avenue Storefront, 6702 Lyons Ave #3, 713-672-5809; Market Street (5th Ward) Storefront, 4300 Lyons Ave, 713-672-5890; Southmore Storefront, 3711 Southmore Blvd, 713-526-1255

Emergency Hospital: St. Joseph's Hospital, 1401 St. Joseph Pkwy, 713-757-1000

Libraries: Houston Public Library, www.hpl.lib.tx.us: Flores Branch, 110 N Milby St, 832-393-1780 (under renovation); Fifth Ward Branch, 4014 Market St, 832-393-1770; Mancuso Branch, 6767 Bellfort St, 832-393-1920

Adult Education: Texas Southern University, www.tsu.edu, 3100 Cleburne St, 713-313-7011; University of Houston, www.uh.edu, 4800 Calhoun Rd, 713-743-2255

Public Education: Houston Independent School District, www.houstonisd.org, 4400 W 18th St, 713-556-6005

Community Publications: Houston Chronicle, www.chron.com; Houston *Defender*, www.defendernetwork.com; Houston Press, www.houstonpress.com

Community Resources: Ninos de la Comunidad, 2805 Garrow St; Third Ward Multi-Service Center, 3611 Ennis St, 713-527-4002; East End Chamber of Commerce, www.eecoc.org, 550 Gulfgate Center, 713-926-3305; Talento Bilingue de Houston, www.talentobilingue.org, 333 S Jensen Dr, 713-222-1213; Our Lady of Guadalupe Church, www.olghouston.org, 2405 Navigation Blvd, 713-222-0203

Public Transportation: Harris County Metropolitan Transit Authority, www.ridemetro.org: *Bus:* 11, 20, 26, 27, 29, 30, 36, 37, 40, 42, 48, 50, 68, 77, 88, 244, 246, 247

MONTROSE

Boundaries: North: Allen Pkwy; **East:** Bagby; **South:** US 59; **West:** Shepherd

To many Houstonians, Montrose is synonymous with the gay community. This funky, alternative neighborhood, however, is home not only to many of the city's gay and lesbian inhabitants, but also to an eclectic mix of college students, artists, young urban professionals, intellectuals, bohemian types, tattoo and piercing enthusiasts, families, and couples.

Montrose's diverse population is a result of its proximity to the Museum District, several small art museums such as the de Menil Museum, St. Thomas University (a private Catholic four-year institution), River Oaks, the Chinese consulate, Midtown and its nightlife, urban lofts, and other single-family residential areas. With Montrose's proximity to so many attractions, there are always plenty of activities and events in the neighborhood. In fact, Montrose is the site of the annual Greek Festival, Westheimer Street Festival, and Gay Pride parade.

Montrose's narrow pedestrian-friendly streets (by Houston standards), unique shops, and open-minded attitude give the area its own character and strong sense of community. Several independently owned coffee houses line these streets and sell coffee from all over the world. Like many of the other colorful local shops in this neighborhood, they espouse an anti-corporate, pro-neighborhood ethos.

Though this neighborhood attracts progressive, open-minded types, as well as gay and lesbian teen runaways, the recent revitalization of downtown and the housing boom of the late 1990s has transformed parts of this neighborhood and increased housing prices. Toward the eastern part of Montrose, near Midtown, new condos and apartments have popped up, replacing the artists and hippies with urban professionals.

Located between downtown and the Texas Medical Center, **Neartown** is a charming neighborhood of predominantly two-story homes of various designs. Independently owned shops line Richmond and major thoroughfares, which tend to be narrow. Neartown is sometimes lumped together with Montrose and also is composed of a unique array of residents, including politicians, businessmen, and medical doctors. Past local luminaries include Howard Hughes, Lyndon B. Johnson, Walter Cronkite, and pioneering heart surgeon Denton Cooley.

In the 1960s, the Neartown association was established to preserve some of the city's oldest and most historic homes. Other neighborhoods in the area such as **Courtlandt Place, Winlow Place, Hyde Park,** and **Cherryhurst** are also old Houston neighborhoods. Newer subdivisions include **Audubon, Avondale, Lancaster Place, Castle Court,** and **Roseland Estates.**

Website: www.cityofhouston.net
Area Code: 713
Zip Code: 77006

Post Offices: University of Houston Station, 1319 Richmond; River Oaks Station, 1900 W Gray St

Police Precinct: Houston Police Department: Neartown Storefront, 802 Westheimer Rd, 713-284-8604

Emergency Hospitals: Christus St. Joseph, www.sjmctx.com, 1401 St. Joseph Pkwy, 713-757-1000; Texas Medical Center, www.tmc.edu: Hermann Hospital, www.memorialhermann.org, 6411 Fannin St, 713-704-4000; Ben Taub, www.hchdonline.com, Ben Taub General Hospital, 1504 Taub Loop, 713-873-2000; Methodist Hospital, www.methodisthealth.com, 6565 Fannin St, 713-790-3311; VA Hospital, 2002 Holcombe Blvd, 1-800-553-2278; St. Luke's, www.sleh.com, 6720 Bertner Ave, 832-355-1000; Texas Children's Hospital, www.texaschildrenshospital.org, 6621 Fannin St, 832-824-1000

Library: Houston Public Library, www.hpl.lib.tx.us: Freed-Montrose Branch, 4100 Montrose Blvd, 832-393-1800

Public Education: Houston Independent School District, www.houstonisd.org, 4400 W 18th St, 713-556-6005

Community Publications: *Houston Chronicle*, www.chron.com; *Houston Press*, www.houstonpress.com

Community Resources: Houston City Hall, 900 Bagby St, 713-837-0311; Cherryhurst Community Center, 1700 Missouri St, 713-284-1992

Public Transportation: Harris County Metropolitan Authority, www.ridemetro.org: *Bus:* 3, 25, 26, 27, 34, 35, 42, 78, 82, 170, 291, 292, 298

BELLAIRE, WEST UNIVERSITY PLACE, SOUTHSIDE PLACE, AND OLD BRAESWOOD

Boundaries: *BELLAIRE:* **North:** US 59; **East:** Southern Pacific Railroad track; **South:** Beechnut/N Braeswood; **West:** Renwick; *WEST UNIVERSITY PLACE:* **North:** University Blvd; **East:** Virginia; **South:** Gramercy; **West:** Auden; *SOUTHSIDE PLACE:* **North:** University; **East:** Edloe; **South:** Gramercy; **West:** Bellaire and Auden; *OLD BRAESWOOD:* **North:** Holcombe Blvd; **East:** Main; **South:** Brays Bayou; **West:** Kirby

Bellaire, West University Place, and Southside Place are a collection of wealthy, independently governed communities with a significant population of medical professionals who work at the nearby Medical Center and professors employed at Rice University. Residents here are zoned to two of the top public high schools in Houston, Bellaire and Lamar. Though you'll find some reasonably priced residences here, property taxes can be quite high.

Bellaire is an affluent bedroom community in southwest Houston that is actually a city (of about 18,000 residents) within a city. Established in 1908, Bellaire was connected by a trolley to Houston, which was then several miles away. The trolley was discontinued in 1927 and today sits on Bellaire Boulevard as a historical exhibit. Houston, however, continued to grow and sprawled westward, eventually surrounding Bellaire. Houston never annexed Bellaire, which is still an independent municipality with its own mayor, city council, police department, fire department, and library. Its schools, however, are part of the Houston Independent School District.

Despite being surrounded by a big city, Bellaire has managed to retain a quiet, small-town, family-friendly ambience. Children often can be seen riding their bikes in the street alongside young couples pushing baby strollers. Each year residents eagerly support their Little League baseball team, which won the 2000 Little League World Series, and their high school baseball team, which has won numerous state championships. Education and children are major focus points of this community.

Bellaire is known as the "City of Homes" because it is primarily a residential area with a combination of '50s-style bungalows, spacious ranch houses, two-story homes, multimillion-dollar mansions that have replaced smaller one-story homes, and a few recently constructed townhomes. There is a current trend of new home-buyers tearing down smaller existing homes and building larger residences, or McMansions, on the site. The city has several independently owned shops, businesses, and offices, but few attractions. Bellaire, however, makes up for its lack of attractions with its proximity to Houston's downtown sports and theater district, the Medical Center, Rice University, the Galleria shopping district, the Museum district, the zoo, Hermann Park, and Reliant football stadium.

Bellaire is also conveniently located near US 59 and Loop 610, which connect the city to Houston and beyond. Add excellent public schools to the Bellaire's geographic location and atmosphere and one can quickly see why it's one of the Houston area's most desirable places to live.

When the first homes in **West University Place** were sold in 1917, its founder, Tennessee Governor Ben W. Hooper, and developer, the Houston West End Realty Company, could not have envisioned how successful the community would

Bellaire

become in the following decades. When development first began, the area was swampy, muddy, and had difficulty attaining utilities—hardly the type of place one would have imagined would one day become one of Houston's most desirable neighborhoods. At the time, its future was uncertain, and Governor Hooper had to use his own money to develop critical infrastructure and utilities after the City of Houston refused to take such a risk. Nevertheless, the residents persisted and voted to incorporate as a city in 1924. By the 1940s West University Place was a thriving community that was a far cry from the once-rural backwater community.

West University Place, also commonly referred to as West University or West U., is named for its location west of Rice University. Like Bellaire, this very wealthy bedroom community located next to it is an independent city (population about 15,000) surrounded by Houston. One of the most charming communities in Houston, it's characterized by beautiful lawns and elegant homes, which include small Tudor cottages, large brick mansions, Colonials, modern designs, and various other architectural styles. Strict deed restrictions have helped preserve the community's aesthetic appeal. Regardless of the street, each home in West University is unique. The neighborhood streets here are narrow, reflecting an era before cities were built around automobiles and before large vehicles played a prominent role in the daily lives of Americans. The layout and design of the neighborhoods promote children playing in the streets and residents stopping and chatting with one another. When people talk about smart urban or community design that is child-friendly and socially oriented, they're probably thinking about someplace like West University.

One of the most popular places in this neighborhood is **Rice Village**, a pedestrian shopping district that spans several blocks. It's a favorite place not only of Rice University students and locals but also of residents from all over Houston. One of Houston's premier shopping districts, Rice Village dates back to the 1930s. Since then it has expanded beyond its original buildings, which still stand today. New brick buildings that blend in with the area's design and a parking garage in the rear have been added to the district. Rice Village is known for its unique boutiques and independently owned shops. Among the more than 300 shops in the Village are also several national clothing chains and retailers in the newer sections.

Visitors looking for someplace to eat have an array of options, including Thai, Japanese, Turkish, Greek, American, Chinese, Spanish, Mexican, and Italian restaurants. On the weekends, the casual bars, pubs, and trendy upscale lounges that mingle side by side are packed with patrons. Parking on the weekends can be a hassle, especially along Morningside and University. Evidently, though, many people believe it's worth it, as witnessed by the crowds here. Across from the Village, on the other side of Kirby Drive, you'll find several townhomes, some of them recently constructed. There are also many rental properties in the West Village that are usually occupied either by university students or medical residents from the Medical Center.

Tucked into West University is an L-shaped area known as **Southside Place.** This very affluent community covers only nine streets, which are in alphabetical order. This secluded neighborhood dates back to the 1920s, when it was a small community. It has the same small-town, family-friendly atmosphere as West University Place and Bellaire. Sometimes it's difficult to tell the difference between West University Place and Southside Place. Almost all of the commercial businesses are located along Bellaire Boulevard/Holcombe, which also runs through West University Place and Bellaire.

The **Old Braeswood** neighborhood dates back to the 1930s and is located across from West University Place on the other side of Holcombe Boulevard. Previously called Braeswood, it was renamed Old Braeswood in the 1980s to distinguish itself from the other neighborhoods, commonly referred to as Braeswood, that were developing along Brays Bayou. Though not one of the most recognizable neighborhoods by name, it rivals Houston's most prestigious residential areas. Homes here steadily have increased in value over the years, and many are now worth $400,000 or more. Old Braeswood is characterized by large trees and historic homes. Its architectural design, street layout, and ambience are similar to West University Place. Some of the old homes, however, slowly are being replaced by large multistory townhomes that appear conspicuously out of place in a quiet residential neighborhood.

Websites: www.ci.bellaire.tx.us, www.westu.org, www.ci.southside-place.tx.us, www.oldbraeswood.com
Area Code: 713
Zip Codes: 77401, 77005, 77025
Post Offices: Bellaire Station, 5350 Bellaire Blvd, Bellaire; William Rice Station, 5201 Wakeforest St, Houston; Astrodome Station, 8205 Braeswood Dr, Houston; Medical Center Station, 7205 Almeda Rd, Houston
Police Departments: Bellaire Police Department, 5110 Jessamine St, Bellaire, 713-668-0487; West University Police Department, 3814 University Blvd, West University Pl, 713-668-0330; Southside Place Police Department, 6309 Edloe Ave, Houston, 713-668-2341; Houston Police Department, South Central Patrol, 2202 St. Emanuel St, Houston, 713-651-8100
Emergency Hospitals: Texas Medical Center, www.tmc.edu: Hermann Hospital, www.memorialhermann.org, 6411 Fannin St, 713-704-4000; Ben Taub, www.hchdonline.com, Ben Taub General Hospital, 1504 Taub Loop, 713-873-2000; Methodist Hospital, www.methodisthealth.com, 6565 Fannin St, 713-790-3311; VA Hospital, www.houston.med.va.gov, 2002 Holcombe Blvd, 1-800-553-2278; St. Luke's, www.sleh.com, 6720 Bertner Ave, 832-355-1000; Texas Children's Hospital, www.texaschildrenshospital.org, 6621 Fannin St, 832-824-1000
Libraries: Bellaire City Library, 5111 Jessamine, Bellaire, 713-662-8166; Harris County Public Library, www.hcpl.net, 6108 Auden, Houston, 713-668-8273
Public Education: Houston Independent School District, www.houstonisd.org, 4400 W 18th St, Houston, 713-556-6005

Community Publications: *Bellaire Examiner* and *West University Examiner*, www.westuexaminer.com

Community Resources: Bellaire City Hall, 7008 S Rice Ave, Bellaire, 713-662-8222; West University Place City Hall, 3800 University Blvd, West University Place, 713-668-4441; Southside Place City Hall, 6309 Edloe Ave, Houston, 713-668-2341; Southwest Chamber of Commerce, www.gswhcc.org, PO Box 788, Bellaire, 713-666-1521

Public Transportation: Metropolitan Transit Authority of Harris County, www.ridemetro.org; *Bus:* 2, 49, 33, 65

MUSEUM/MEDICAL CENTER
Rice University Area/Museum District/Texas Medical Center

Boundaries: North: US 59; **East:** Hwy 288; **South:** Old Spanish Trail and Braeswood; **West:** Greenbriar

One of the loveliest parts of Houston, the area that surrounds Rice University is popular with joggers and visitors, who enjoy its shaded trees and beautiful landscape. The Rice University Area's most distinctive characteristic is the canopy of oak trees that line South Main Street and other parts of the community. The area is beautiful year 'round, but the most gorgeous time of the year is spring, when the azaleas and other flowers come into full bloom. The spectacular Mecom Fountain display, which sits in the center of South Main, forms the city's only major traffic circle. One fork of this road takes drivers directly to the Museum District, another heads toward Montrose, and another toward downtown. Within walking distance of one another are the Museum of Fine Arts, Contemporary Arts Museum, and the Museum of Natural Science. Also nearby are the Rothko Chapel, de Menil Museum, Holocaust Museum, the Children's Museum of Houston, and other art galleries. Right across from the university is the Houston Zoo, Hermann Park, the Botanical Gardens, and the Museum of Natural Science. Hermann Park, a natural oasis amid the traffic and noise of the city, is one of Houston's most tranquil and well-maintained parks, due in large part to the nonprofit Hermann Park Conservancy. A small number of high-rise condominiums that overlook the park are located across from this area, and the Museum District as a whole contains many luxury condominiums. The first light rail system, called the Red Line, stops in front of the park and runs straight between downtown and the South Main/610 Loop area.

Modern contemporary, traditional, antebellum, Colonial, bungalow, Tudor, Mediterranean, Italianate, and other uniquely designed homes are hidden in the streets off South Main. The individuality of the houses contributes character and appeal to this safe and peaceful community. Some homes are more exclusive and hidden among shady oak trees behind lightly ivy-covered walls. In recent years the university has constructed several apartments and dorms for international students, graduate students, and families in the neighborhoods. The neighborhoods in this area include:

- **Southampton:** Developed in 1922, this neighborhood features many older large bungalows and Georgian-style residences with some new construction of million-dollar homes.
- **Southgate:** This neighborhood is bordered by West Holcombe on the south, Greenbriar on the west, University on the north, and Travis on the west. Most of the homes here were built in the 1930s and 1940s.
- **Boulevard Oaks:** Bounded by the Southwest Freeway (US 59) on the north, Morningside on the west, Bissonet on the south, and Graustark/Parkway on the east, this neighborhood is surrounded by beautiful landscape. Developed in the 1920s and 1930s, Boulevard Oaks' diverse architectural styles include bungalows, ranch-style homes, and mansions.

Medical Center and South Loop Area (Astrodome/Reliant Center)

The area that surrounds the Medical Center contains many apartments and townhomes, most of which are located along Braeswood. The rentals here are fairly recent and are usually large multi-building complexes that cater to medical students, interns, and residents. Many of the Medical Center employees and medical students also live around the Astrodome area, located farther down South Main and Fannin. This was a rundown area until the development of the light rail and the building of the new Reliant football stadium initiated the area's revitalization. The area immediately next to Reliant Stadium currently is comprised of affordable, low-rise apartments, while on the other side of the stadium several new apartments and townhomes have sprung up over the past few years as developers saw an opportunity with the increased demand for in-town housing and the completion of the light rail. Though there are still pockets of eyesore, the area has steadily improved and more development is expected in the future.

Medical Center

BRAESWOOD PLACE

Boundaries: North: Southside and West University Pl; **East:** Southern Pacific Railroad; **South:** Brays Bayou; **West:** Old Braeswood neighborhood

Primarily a single-family residential neighborhood developed in the 1950s, Braeswood Place is one of several neighborhoods and subdivisions that line Brays Bayou. The others are located outside of the 610 Loop. Because of its location next to the bayou, flooding can be a problem for residents. During Tropical Storm Allison in 2001, many of the small ranch-style homes that predominated before the storm were flooded out and had to be torn down. Larger two-story homes built on higher foundations have replaced the ranch houses. Generally a middle-class neighborhood before the flood, Braeswood Place has seen more upper-middle-income families moving into the newer homes constructed after Allison. Subdivisions here include **Ayrshire**, **Braes Heights**, **Braes Manor**, **Braes Oaks**, **Braes Terrace**, and **Southern Oaks**.

Stella Link/Linkwood

Just inside the Loop, the Linkwood neighborhood features one-story ranch-style homes with low-slung roofs. Homes here have large front and back yards.

Websites: www.houstontx.gov, www.braeswoodplace.org, www.houstonsouthgate.org
Area Code: 713
Zip Codes: 77005, 77030, 77054, 77025, 77098
Post Offices: William Rice Station, 5201 Wakeforest St; Medical Center Station, 7205 Almeda Rd; Greenbriar Station, 3740 Greenbriar St
Police Departments: Houston Police Department: South Central Division, 2202 St. Emanuel St, 713-651-8100; Central Division, 61 Riesner St, 713-247-4400; Rice University Police Department MS-551, 6100 Main St, 713-348-6000; University of Texas Medical Center Police, 1515 Holcombe Blvd, 713-792-2890
Emergency Hospitals: Texas Medical Center, www.tmc.edu: Hermann Hospital, www.memorialhermann.org, 6411 Fannin St, 713-704-4000; Ben Taub, www.hchdonline.com, Ben Taub General Hospital, 1504 Taub Loop, 713-873-2000; Methodist Hospital, www.methodisthealth.com, 6565 Fannin St, 713-790-3311; VA Hospital, 2002 Holcombe Blvd, 800-553-2278; St. Luke's, www.sleh.com, 6720 Bertner Ave, 832-355-1000; Texas Children's Hospital, www.texaschildrenshospital.org, 6621 Fannin St, 832-824-1000
Libraries: Houston Public Library, McGovern–Stella Link Branch, 7405 Stella Link Rd, 832-393-2630; Clayton Library Center for Genealogical Research, 5300 Caroline, 832-393-2600; Parent Resource Library in the Children's Museum, 1500 Binz St, 713-522-1138 ext. 264; Rice University Fondren Library, 6100 Main St, 713-348-5113; Houston Academy of Medicine–Texas Medical Center Library, 1133 John Freeman Blvd, 713-795-4200

Adult Education: Rice University, www.rice.edu, 6100 Main St, 713-348-7423
Public Education: Houston Independent School District, www.houstonisd.org, 4400 W 18th St, 713-556-6005
Community Publications: *Houston Chronicle,* www.chron.com; *Houston Press,* www.houstonpress.com; *The Rice Thresher,* ricethresher.org
Community Resources: City Hall, 900 Bagby St, 713-837-0311; Greater Houston YMCA, www.ymcahouston.org: Texas Medical Center Childcare, 5614 H Mark Croswell Jr. St, 713-747-2173; MD Anderson YMCA, 705 Cavalcade St, 713-697-0648; Weekley Family YMCA, 7101 Stella Link Rd, 713-664-9622; Hermann Park, 6001 Fannin St; Miller Outdoor Theater, www.milleroutdoortheater.org, 100 Concert Dr, 713-284-8354; Museum District, www.houstonmuseumdistrict.org
Public Transportation: Metropolitan Authority of Harris County, www.ridemetro.org: Light Rail; *Bus:* 292, 298, 8, 34, 87, 326, 321, 322, 320, 73, 27, 26, 65, 132, 163, 292, 297, 1, 65, 60, 68, 170, 4, 10, 14, 73, 2; Rice University Shuttle

RIVER OAKS/UPPER KIRBY/GREENWAY PLAZA

Boundaries: *RIVER OAKS*: **North**: Buffalo Bayou; **East:** Shepherd; **South:** US 59; **West:** Loop 610; *UPPER KIRBY:* **North:** Westheimer; **East:** Shepherd; **South:** Westpark; **West:** Buffalo Speedway; *GREENWAY PLAZA:* **North:** Richmond; **East:** Shepherd; **South:** US 59; West: Loop 610

River Oaks

River Oaks has a reputation as Houston's poshest neighborhood—the location the city's crème de la crème call home. Many residences here are lavishly elegant, and all of them have beautiful front and back yards. This neighborhood contains a combination of stately mansions, single-family residential homes, luxury condominiums, and recently constructed townhomes. Some of the million-dollar estates are hidden from view behind gates. The neighborhood shows off its homes and gardens each year during the annual Azalea Trail. This springtime event showcases the beautiful flowers in all shades of pink that grace the select residences on this tour.

Highland Village Area

Around the upscale Highland Village shopping center on Westheimer lie several affluent neighborhoods. Many of them are located behind high brick walls that shield residents from the busy traffic on Westheimer. Neighborhoods here include **Afton Oaks, Oak Estates, Avalon Place,** and **Royden Oaks.** Homes vary from newly constructed two-story red brick homes to older elegant residences. Regardless of the age or size, the homes here are all lovely and very expensive. Behind Highland Village you'll find more splendid homes with lavish yards, including Mediterranean-inspired designs and other large homes that are almost mansions.

Because of its location inside the Loop and right next to Westheimer, one of the city's major thoroughfares, and Loop 610, homes here are coveted. Residents have the advantage of being within walking distance of one of the city's best shopping centers, Highland Village, where the stores and restaurants are closely packed together, facilitating a pedestrian shopping experience.

Upper Kirby

Upper Kirby is hard to pin down. It's trendy, upscale, a bit unconventional, and refined all at once. The red British telephone booths scattered throughout the neighborhood are an easy giveaway that you're in Upper Kirby. These booths are in line with the British theme the neighborhood has adopted to go with Upper Kirby's initials, U.K. Another indication that you're in Upper Kirby is the red street signs, rather than the usual green ones. Upper Kirby is a popular entertainment area full of pubs, bars, and a wide selection of restaurants and trendy hangout spots, which can make parking difficult on the weekends. This cosmopolitan area mixes its commercial district with residential neighborhoods that include elegant homes, apartments, and townhomes.

Greenway Plaza Area

Greenway Plaza is the name of a cluster of tall office buildings located off US 59 (Southwest Freeway). Until the past decade, the area around it consisted mainly of business buildings with plots of green grass surrounding them. In the past few years, however, residential development has swallowed up the undeveloped land, and there are no more open patches of grass. Most of the construction here has been luxury apartments, corporate rentals, townhomes, a few lofts, and condominiums. Strip centers, shops, and other businesses have opened up alongside the new residences. No longer a commercial wasteland, Greenway Plaza slowly is evolving into a viable residential area with amenities located nearby. Sushi restaurants, banks, dry cleaners, and take-out joints are all nearby. Travel farther down Buffalo Speedway, under the Southwest Freeway, into the edge of West University, and you'll find a large upscale shopping center with a flagship grocery store, coffee shops, numerous restaurants, cell phone stores, and many other businesses. In addition, residents who live around Greenway Plaza are near the shopping, dining, and entertainment of West University and Upper Kirby. The area's location next to the freeway provides easy access to other parts of Houston.

Websites: www.upperkirbydistrict.org, www.houstontx.gov
Area Code: 713
Zip Codes: 77098, 77019, 77046

Post Offices: River Oaks Station, 1900 W Gray St; Greenbriar Station, 3740 Greenbriar St; Greenway Plaza Station, 3 E Greenway Plaza; Julius Melcher Station, 2802 Timmons Lane; Neartown (Montrose) Storefront, 802 Westheimer Rd

Police Precinct: Houston Police Department: Central Division, 61 Riesner St, 713-247-4400

Emergency Hospitals: Texas Medical Center, www.tmc.edu: Hermann Hospital, www.memorialhermann.org, 6411 Fannin St, 713-704-4000; Ben Taub, www.hchdonline.com, Ben Taub General Hospital, 1504 Taub Loop, 713-873-2000; Methodist Hospital, www.methodisthealth.com, 6565 Fannin St, 713-790-3311; VA Hospital, 2002 Holcombe Blvd, 1-800-553-2278; St. Luke's, www.sleh.com, 6720 Bertner Ave, 832-355-1000; Texas Children's Hospital, www.texaschildrenshospital.org, 6621 Fannin St, 832-824-1000

Libraries: Houston Public Library, www.hpl.lib.tx.us: Looscan Branch, 2510 Willowick Rd; Freed-Montrose Branch, 4100 Montrose Blvd, 832-393-1800

Public Education: Houston Independent School District, www.houstonisd.org, 4400 W 18th St, 713-556-6005

Community Publications: Houston Chronicle, www.chron.com; Houston Press, www.houstonpress.com

Community Resources: City Hall, 900 Bagby St, 713-837-0311; River Oaks Community Center, 3600 Locke Lane, 713-622-5998

Public Transportation: Metropolitan Transit Authority of Harris County, www.ridemetro.org: *Bus:* 65, 132, 163, 25, 78, 82, 35, 18, 35, 3, 6, 70, 48, 34, 42, 9, 27

OUTER LOOP

Also known as "outside the Loop," the Outer Loop refers to any place outside of Loop 610. Residents often ask whether one lives "inside the Loop" or "outside the Loop" to gauge whether someone is centrally located. The Outer Loop consists primarily of residential neighborhoods and suburban areas. Though lacking in the cultural attractions and entertainment of the Inner Loop, the areas beyond Loop 610 offer many unique and excellent dining options.

UPTOWN

Uptown, also commonly known as the Galleria area, is an upscale district surrounded by high-end designer stores, hotels, and business towers. It is centered around Houston's premier shopping center, the Galleria. This shoppers' mecca and the other shopping centers nearby feature couture shops and designer brands, as well as more generic, recognizable national clothing retailers. Its location next to tony River Oaks probably explains the proliferation of designer goods and fancy retailers. Uptown has always been an upscale area, but in recent years it has become even more image-conscious. Though Houston is generally a down-to-earth town and eschews pretentiousness, this is one part of the city where you'll find well-dressed yuppies and the high maintenance crowd.

Uptown, primarily the Galleria, is a big tourist destination, especially for those coming from Mexico and South America to buy the latest American and European designer fashions. The huge selection of restaurants here includes Japanese, Italian, American, Tex-Mex, Chinese, Thai, Middle Eastern, Mediterranean, and Indian cuisines, ranging in price and ambience from casual to upscale. During major events Houston has hosted, such as the Super Bowl and NBA All-Star event, the Galleria has been the place most visited by tourists and party-goers. One of the most popular events here is the Uptown tree-lighting ceremony held on Thanksgiving evening.

When the Galleria was constructed approximately 30 years ago, Uptown was a mostly undeveloped suburban area. The 1970s oil boom, however, increased the city's population and soon spurred residential development here. Many Houstonians' bank accounts increased, providing them with enough money to spend on luxury goods at the Galleria. As a result, the Uptown area has experienced a second residential development boom. Much of it started in the 1990s, when the economy was on an upswing, and continued because of low mortgage interest rates and an increased demand for housing near the city's center. Empty grass lots behind the Galleria have been completely filled in by the mall's expansion and the construction of new townhomes and shopping strips. More recently, the area has seen a flurry of construction of high-rise condominiums, lofts, townhomes, and a few luxury apartments.

With its steel and glass buildings, sleek new metallic street signs, contemporary-style bus stops, and busy street and pedestrian traffic, Uptown has a sophisticated, cosmopolitan feel. The most notable building here and in all of Houston is the Williams Tower, formerly the Transco Tower. Designed by famed architect Phillip Johnson, it features a water tower in the backdrop and a park at the front. This 64-story landmark skyscraper, constructed of blue glass, stands out in an area where buildings are typically mid- or low-rise. Because of its height, the Williams Tower serves as a reference point in a city with a very flat landscape. The nearer the tower appears, the closer you are to the Galleria area.

The strip down Westheimer and Richmond until Westchase often is referred to as the Galleria area even though it is not immediately near the Galleria. The main thoroughfares are blocks of strip shopping centers and popular restaurants. Step off Westheimer and Richmond and you'll find many quiet residential neighborhoods nestled amid leafy trees. These neighborhoods include luxury townhomes and large one-story ranch-style homes with big yards.

TANGLEWOOD/BRIARGROVE

Tanglewood is a close-in affluent neighborhood similar to Memorial and River Oaks. Though technically outside Loop 610, this wealthy enclave located near the

Uptown/Galleria area is conveniently near Loop 610, Memorial/Woodway, and other major thoroughfares that lead to the city's business centers and amenities—so much so that it is like living in-town. At the same time, Tanglewood has a tranquil country-setting atmosphere that is not infringed upon by its proximity to the hustle and bustle of the city. Arching oak trees line the neighborhood's streets, and tall trees shade many of the properties here. The elegant luxury houses are uniquely designed and include Georgian, contemporary, and chateau-inspired homes. They range from large estates to low-maintenance garden homes. Several years ago developers began tearing down many of the one-story residences on large, heavily treed lots and built magnificent residences in their place. These include large homes in traditional, Georgian, and Mediterranean styles. Home to the Houston Country Club, Tanglewood is one of Houston's most exclusive areas. Its most famous resident is former US President George H.W. Bush. Other residents, however, have more mundane backgrounds, mostly families of business executives and other professionals. Home prices and property taxes here are at the high end of the Houston housing market. Tanglewood was developed in the 1940s from prairie land into a beautiful and heavily treed neighborhood. Over the years, high-end retailers and restaurants have moved nearby. **Briargrove** enjoys many of the same amenities but offers more modestly priced housing.

Websites: www.houstontx.gov, www.uptown-houston.com
Area Code: 713
Zip Codes: 77056, 77057
Post Offices: Galleria Station, 5015 Westheimer Rd, Ste 1200; CPU Tanglewood Pharmacy Station, 5750 Woodway Dr, Ste 156
Police Precinct: Houston Police Department: Central Division, 61 Riesner St, 713-247-4400

Tanglewood

HOUSTON: OUTER LOOP

Emergency Hospitals: Texas Medical Center, www.tmc.edu: Hermann Hospital, www.memorialhermann.org, 6411 Fannin St, 713-704-4000; Ben Taub, www.hchdonline.com, Ben Taub General Hospital, 1504 Taub Loop, 713-873-2000; Methodist Hospital, www.methodisthealth.com, 6565 Fannin St, 713-790-3311; VA Hospital, www.houston.med.va.gov, 2002 Holcombe Blvd, 1-800-553-2278; St. Luke's, www.sleh.com, 6720 Bertner Ave, 832-355-1000; Texas Children's Hospital, www.texaschildrenshospital.org, 6621 Fannin St, 832-824-1000
Library: Houston Public Library, Jungman Branch, 5830 Westheimer Rd, 832-393-1860
Public Education: Houston Independent School District, www.houstonisd.org, 4400 W 18th St, 713-556-6005
Community Publications: *Houston Chronicle*, www.chron.com; *Houston Press*, www.houstonpress.com
Community Resources: City Hall, 900 Bagby St, 713-837-0311
Public Transportation: Metropolitan Transit Authority of Harris County, www.ridemetro.org: *Bus:* 6, 25, 33, 35, 49, 53, 70, 73

WESTCHASE

Westchase is primarily a commercial district located along Westheimer Road and Beltway 8. Gleaming glass office towers and strip centers line parts of Beltway 8, which is the feeder road for the Sam Houston Tollway. The tollway provides quick access to I-10, US 290, US 59, and other parts of the Houston metropolitan area. Traffic can be very bad around here during rush hour because both the Beltway and Westheimer are major thoroughfares. Parts of Beltway 8 are quite unattractive and resemble nothing more than massive stretches of concrete. There are several apartments and townhomes in the area, mostly on Westheimer, west of the Beltway. Off Westheimer are several secluded single-family residential neighborhoods, including **Rivercrest, Briar Grove Park,** and **Briar Court** east of the Beltway, and **Lakeside Country Club, Walnut Bend, Lakeside Estates, Village West,** and **Royal Palms** to the west of Beltway 8. Homes here are located among lush vegetation and quiet scenic settings. Residents can choose from several chain restaurants and outstanding dining establishments that include international cuisine from Malaysia/Indonesia, Japan, France, South America, and Great Britain.

Websites: www.houstontx.gov, www.westchasedistrict.com, www.briargrovepark.org, www.lakesidecc.com, www.rivercrestestates.com, www.royaloakscc.com, www.walnutbend.org,
Area Codes: 713, 281
Zip Codes: 77042, 77063
Post Offices: Debora Sue Schatz Station, 2909 Rogerdale Rd; Westchase Station, 3836 S Gessner Rd

Police Precincts: Houston Police Department: Clarkcrest Storefront, 8940 Clarkcrest St, 713-952-0182; Southwest Patrol, 4503 Beechnut St, 713-314-3900
Emergency Hospital: West Houston Medical Center, www.westhoustonmedical.com, 12141 Richmond Ave, 281-558-3444
Library: Houston Public Library, www.hpl.lib.tx.us: Robinson-Westchase Branch, 3223 Wilcrest Dr, 832-393-2011
Public Education: Houston Independent School District, www.houstonisd.org, 4400 W 18th St, 713-556-6005 (north of Westheimer Rd); Alief Independent School District, www.aliefisd.net, 12302 High Star Dr, 281-498-8110 (south of Westheimer Rd)
Community Publication: *Houston Chronicle*, www.chron.com
Community Resource: West Houston Association, www.westhouston.org, 820 Gessner Rd, Ste 190, 713-461-9378
Public Transportation: Harris County Metropolitan Transit Authority, www.metro.org: *Bus:* 2, 25, 46, 82, 132, 274

THE MEMORIAL AREA

Memorial is one of Houston's most prestigious areas. This wealthy community is distinguished by the towering pine trees, tall moss-covered oaks, and lush vegetation that create a forest-like ambience. Fed by the waters of Buffalo Bayou, the trees in this area are mature and grander than in any other part of Houston. Memorial is highly sought-after for its beauty, location, and quality of life. In addition, the community is known for good public schools at both the elementary and secondary level.

Memorial is an established community that dates back to the 1930s; residences here once sat on large expanses with horse stables in the rear. Memorial was where the wealthy kept country estates. At that time it was a popular area for horseback riding, and riders often could be seen jaunting through the forested acres. Over the years the large estates have been sold and divided for residential development. One of the last private stables in the area, along South Gessner, was sold in the early 1990s and turned into a gated upscale residential development. The area is more densely populated now, but it still has managed to retain its arboreal environment. Many of the streets follow the contours of the bayou and feel like winding country lanes. The homes here vary in size and style from bungalows to fairytale cottages to brick Georgian residences. Memorial is not the type of place where you'll find cookie-cutter neighborhoods with tract housing. Here, houses of individual designs sit next to each other. There are also many gated communities, condominiums, and townhomes.

The jewel of the Memorial area is Memorial Park, which is just inside the Loop, immediately east of Memorial and next to the Inner Loop neighborhood of Rice Military (see the section on **Rice Military/Camp Logan/Crestwood** for more information about Memorial Park).

Memorial

Memorial is comprised of several neighborhoods and subdivisions, such as **Woodlake/Woodlake Square** located along Gessner. It features gated townhome communities. Farther down Gessner, it is difficult to miss the huge brick structure that marks the **Teal Wood** neighborhood, a portion of which lies in Bunker Hill Village. Just east of Gessner and south of Memorial Drive, **Whispering Oaks** and **Warrenton** are two lovely neighborhoods established in the late 1950s and early 1960s. Some of the homes here are perched at the edge of a bluff and have dramatic backyard views of the bayou below. Warrenton and a portion of Whispering Oaks are located in Bunker Hill. Another lovely nearby neighborhood is **Sandlewood**. This beautiful lakeside neighborhood features large, old shade trees. Hidden among towering trees between Buffalo Bayou and Memorial Drive, this private neighborhood features three manmade lakes that date as far back as 100 years. The banks of the bayou, lake, and the woods provide wonderful places for residents to walk or jog.

The Villages

Within Memorial are several tiny incorporated self-governing municipalities that refer to themselves as villages. Some of these villages, with their small geographic coverage, small population, close community, and wooded environment, definitely have a country village or small-town atmosphere. The Memorial Villages are some of the most affluent parts of Houston and have a large concentration of wealth packed into just a few square miles. These villages of are some of the nicest residential areas with some of the most spectacular homes in Houston. They are surrounded by beautiful natural scenery of the woods and bayou, offer excellent public schools, and are in proximity to Houston's business centers, major freeways, and local attractions. Bunker Hill Village, Hedwig Village, Piney Point, and Hunters Creek are located south of I-10, and Hillshire Village and Spring Valley are located north of I-10.

A charmingly quaint incorporated village, **Bunker Hill Village** is a highly sought-after residential neighborhood. Protected from the worries of the outside world by a forest of towering trees, life here seems almost idyllic. Concerns about annexation by Houston and possible loss of its quiet country-style atmosphere led residents to incorporate the area in the 1950s. A little more than 1,000 families live in enormous homes that cover these few square miles bounded by Taylorcrest Lane to the north, Blalock to the east, Memorial Drive to the south, and the City of Houston to the west.

Hedwig Village is named after Hedwig Jankowski Shroeder, a German immigrant who was the original owner of part of the land that is the present site of the village. Ms. Shroeder came to the US in 1906 and purchased the land, which she later donated to the county for a right of way. The area was incorporated in 1954 and is the smallest of the Memorial Villages. It is located immediately north of Bunker Hill Village and Piney Point Village, south of I-10, west of Hunters Creek Village, and east of the City of Houston. Unlike most of the other villages, which contain only residences, Hedwig Village has its own commercial zone that features banks, groceries, and other amenities. Nearby Katy Freeway (I-10) and the Sam Houston Tollway provide easy access to the city's business centers and attractions.

The area that is now incorporated as **Hunters Creek** was originally settled by German farmers who later established a sawmill. Some of the homes here were built by the people who worked at the sawmill, which no longer exists. In the past few years, several new residential developments have been constructed. Many of the homes built in the 1960s have been torn down and replaced with magnificent custom-built homes. Bounded by I-10 to the north, the City of Houston to the east, Buffalo Bayou to the south, and Piney Point Village to the west, Hunters Creek is one of the larger villages.

Piney Point covers 2.5 square miles of heavily forested area devoted solely to single-family residential homes. Businesses are restricted from operating within this village. In the early 1930s, Piney Point still was considered the far west of Houston, where many people from the city had weekend country homes. After Memorial Drive developed into a major thoroughfare in the 1950s, Houston began growing westward. Fearing annexation by the city, Piney Point residents incorporated their community in 1954. Its boundaries are the City of Hunters Creek to the north and east, Buffalo Bayou and Piney Point Gully to the south, and Blalock to the west.

The smallest of the incorporated villages, **Hillshire Village** is bounded by Westview to the north, Wirt Road to the east, I-10 to the south, and Spring Branch Bayou/city limits of Spring Valley to the west.

Spring Valley

Spring Valley residents incorporated their community in 1955, primarily to have zoning, which the City of Houston does not have. It is solely a single-family residential community. Spring Valley lies west of Hillshire Village, north of I-10, east of the City of Houston, and south of Spring Branch Bayou.

Briar Forest

This neighborhood is definitely forest-like. At one time it served as a Boy Scout camp, but today large residences and mansions are tucked behind heavily wooded areas and lush green vegetation. Though many of the homes date back to the 1970s, when development in the area began, there also has been recent construction on once undeveloped wooded acres near Briar Forest Road. Many of the newer homes are extravagant estates in the Mediterranean style with red tile roofs, tennis courts, and swimming pools. Older residences are quite large as well and beautifully elegant. Roads here are narrow and resemble quiet country lanes. A peaceful community set among towering pines, Briar Forest offers country-like living but is surprisingly close to major arteries such as Beltway 8, and along the major thoroughfare of Briar Forest Road.

Memorial West

Beyond Beltway 8 is Memorial West, which consists of newer residential developments. The farther west you travel, the newer the communities you'll see. Carved out of Memorial's pristine forests, it has much of the lush vegetation and ancient towering trees that provide a great deal of the ambience and character of the Memorial area. Memorial West includes the Energy Corridor, the area along I-10 between Beltway 8 and Grand Parkway where many energy companies including British Petroleum, Shell Exploration, ExxonMobil Chemical, and Conoco Phillips have offices. It lies near the Addicks/Barker, Bear Creek, and Mission Bend communities. Homes here are similar to those in Memorial.

Spring Branch

Just northwest of Memorial is **Spring Branch**, originally established as a religious community settled by German farmers in the 1830s. Like Memorial, it has a similar natural environment of lush flora and tall shady trees. Spring Branch, however, is less upscale and more diverse than Memorial. Its large Hispanic population has replaced many of the original white residents. In addition, the Korean community has opened up many commercial businesses here.

Websites: www.houstontx.gov, www.springvalleytx.com, www.cityofhunterscreek.com, www.cityofpineypoint.com, www.thecityofhedwigvillage.com, www.bunkerhill.net
Area Codes: 713, 281
Zip Codes: 77055, 77063, 77024

Post Offices: Long Point Station, 8000 Long Point Rd; John Dunlop Station, 8728 Beverlyhill St; Memorial Park Station, 10505 Town and Country Way; Rich Hill Station, 2950 Unity Dr; James Griffith Station, 9320 Emnora Lane

Police Precincts: Houston Police Department: Spring Branch Storefront, 8400 Long Point Rd #A, 713-464-6901; Gessner Storefront, 1331 Gessner Rd, 713-772-7691; Memorial Villages Police Department, www.mvpdtx.org, 11981 Memorial Dr, 713-365-3700; Hedwig Village Police Department, 6000 Gaylord Dr; Spring Valley Police Department, 1025 Campbell Rd, 713-465-8323

Emergency Hospitals: Memorial City Hospital, www.memorialhermann.org, 921 Gessner Rd, 713-242-3000; Spring Branch Medical Center, www.springbranchmedical.com, 8850 Long Point, 713-467-6555

Libraries: Harris County Public Library, www.hcpl.net: Spring Branch Memorial Library, 930 Corbindale Rd, 713-464-1633; Houston Public Library, www.hpl.lib.tx.us: Ring Branch, 8835 Long Point Rd, 832-393-2000

Adult Education: Houston Community College, www.hccs.cc.tx.us, Town and Country Center Campus, 1010 W Sam Houston Pkwy N, 713-718-5700

Public Education: Spring Branch Independent School District, www.springbranchisd.com, 955 Campbell Rd, 713-464-1511; Houston Independent School District, www.houstonisd.org, 4400 W 18th St, 713-556-6005 (small parts of Briar Forest subdivision)

Community Publications:, *Houston Chronicle*, www.chron.com; *Houston Press*, www.houstonpress.com

Community Resources: Memorial Park, 6501 Memorial Dr, 713-845-1000

Public Transportation: Harris County Metropolitan Transit Authority, www.metro.org: *Bus:* 6, 46, 70, 131

KATY AND THE KATY AREA

Old Town Katy, as the **City of Katy** is commonly known, is a small agricultural town and former rail town 25 miles west of downtown Houston. It has a small-town atmosphere (population just over 14,000) with the convenience of a major city nearby. Originally called Cane Island, Old Town Katy is located north of I-10 and was settled in the 1830s when the Missouri-Kansas-Texas railroad passed through the area. The main agricultural crop here was and still is rice. In honor of its primary cash crop, the city holds an annual Rice Harvest Festival. In 1934, oil was discovered in this area, and the Humble (now Exxon) Oil Company built a plant out here. Old Town Katy is often confused with the Katy Area, a series of suburban developments to the east that are not all within the City of Katy's boundaries. Main attractions here are the Katy Mills Mall and the Forbidden Gardens, a miniature replica of China that covers the country's culture and history.

The **Katy Area**, where most of the new development is taking place, is located east of the City of Katy along I-10 and US Highway 90, in parts of Harris, Waller, and

Katy

Fort Bend counties. The Katy Area has grown tremendously in the last 20 years into a major suburb. Many of the older Katy neighborhoods still exist and feature mostly very affordable single-story homes. The new master-planned residential developments, however, are what attract families here. These include new developments such as **Cinco Ranch** and **Grand Lakes** and older developments from the 1970s and 1980s, such as **Memorial Parkway** and **Nottingham Country**. Cinco Ranch is a large, affluent, master-planned community that includes the most up-to-date amenities. Within the community is an artificial beach that surrounds a large, shallow community swimming pool and a well-maintained golf course. Grand Lakes is a similar but smaller master-planned development with central parks, recreation centers, pools, spray parks, tennis courts, playgrounds, and putting greens. New residences are mostly dark brick homes that vary in size but are almost identical in style. Many of the neighborhoods in Grand Lakes feature large subdivisions of tract houses. With plenty of open space, homes are relatively affordable and there is still plenty of new construction in the Katy Area.

Most of the development is the result of the expansion of the Energy Corridor along I-10 West. Residents have two of the largest urban parks, George Bush and Cullen/Bear Creek, for jogging, rollerblading, and cycling. These parks also have soccer fields, picnic sites, nature trails, dog parks, a velodrome, and skeet and clay pigeon shooting facilities. The quiet residential streets, good public schools, and proximity to nature are the primary reasons residents choose the Katy area despite the traffic on I-10, which once had had the worst gridlock in the metropolitan area. The freeway has been expanded to deal with the increasing population, easing headaches for commuters.

One of the other main distinctions between the City of Katy and the Katy Area is that the Katy Area lies within an unincorporated district that is controlled by the City of Houston, which has the ability to annex it.

Websites: www.cincoranch.com, www.energycorridor.org, www.westfieldkaty.org, www.ci.katy.tx.us
Area Codes: 281, 832
Zip Codes: 77449, 77450, 77493, 77494
Post Offices: Katy Station, 20180 Park Row Dr; Katy Annex Station, 1331 Pin Oak Rd; Katy Finance Station, 5701 4th St
Emergency Hospital: Memorial Hermann Katy Hospital, www.memorialhermann.org, 5602 Medical Center Dr, 281-392-1111
Libraries: Harris County Public Library, www.hcpl.net: Katy Branch, 5414 Franz Rd, 281-391-3509; Maud Smith Marks Branch, 1815 Westgreen Blvd; Fort Bend County Public Library, Cinco Ranch Branch, www.fortbend.lib.tx.us, 2620 Commercial Center Blvd, 281-395-1311
Adult Education: University of Houston at Cinco Ranch, www.cincoranch.uh.edu, 4242 South Mason Rd, 832-842-2800; Houston Community College, Katy Mills, 25403 Kingsland Blvd, 281-644-6080; Houston Community College, Cinco Ranch, 4242 South Mason Rd, 713-718-5757
Public Education: Katy Independent School District, www.katyisd.org, 6301 S Stadium Lane, 281-396-6000
Community Publications: *Katy Times*, www.katytimes.com; *Katy Sun*
Community Resource: Katy Area Chamber of Commerce, www.katychamber.com, 2501 S Mason Rd, Ste 230, 281-828-1100
Public Transportation: Harris County Metropolitan Transit Authority, www.metro.org, *Bus:* 131, 221, 298 (Park and Ride)

ADDICKS/BARKER

Farther west on I-10, between the Barker Reservoir and Addicks Reservoir, are several recent residential neighborhoods known collectively as Addicks/Barker. This

Addicks

area encompasses the **Bear Creek** subdivisions and **Bear Creek Park**. Homes here are designed in various styles and sizes, but almost all are constructed of the same red brick, which tends to dilute the differences in the design of the homes and make them look nearly identical. The Addicks/Barker area was largely rural and densely forested before new home construction, which is still going on, began. Its location far from the city or major commercial areas has resulted in quiet neighborhoods and affordable homes. Two major features of this community are its large reservoirs, Barker and Addicks, which border the neighborhoods. They were built when this part of Houston was a rural area far removed from the city.

Though Addicks is considered a suburb of Houston, it was actually a small, unincorporated town before it was swallowed up by sprawl. Its history dates back to the 1850s, when German immigrants settled the area. Destroyed during the 1900 Galveston hurricane, the town rebuilt. Addicks was relocated in the mid 1940s when the Addicks Dam Reservoir was constructed to protect Houston from floods.

Website: www.co.harris.tx.us
Area Codes: 281, 832
Zip Codes: 77079, 77084
Post Offices: Ashford West Station, 12655 Whittington Dr; Fleetwood Station, 315 Addicks Howell Rd; Bear Creek Station, 16015 Cairnway Dr; Addicks Barker Station, 16830 Barker Springs Rd, Ste 401
Emergency Hospital: West Houston Medical Center, www.westhoustonmedical.com, 12141 Richmond Ave, 281-558-3444
Library: Harris County Public Library, www.hcpl.net: Katherine Tyra Branch at Bear Creek, 16719 Clay Rd, 281-550-0885
Public Education: Katy Independent School District, www.katyisd.org, 6301 S Stadium Lane, Katy, 281-396-6000
Community Publication: *Houston Chronicle*, www.chron.com
Community Resource: Katy Area Chamber of Commerce, www.katychamber.com, 2501 S Mason Rd, Ste 230, Katy, 281-828-1100
Public Transportation: Harris County Metropolitan Transit Authority, www.metro.org: *Bus:* 131, 221, 228, 298 (Park and Ride)

SOUTHWEST HOUSTON

Perhaps the most diverse part of the city, Southwest Houston contains a variety of ethnic communities, religions, and socioeconomic levels. In addition to longtime residents, the southwest area is home to many immigrants from Asia, Africa, Latin America, and the former Soviet Union. You are unlikely to find such a mix of people of different races and varying backgrounds in any other part of Houston. Practitioners of different religions should not have difficulty finding a place of worship here, due to the area's many churches, some of which cater to a specific ethnic community or language; several synagogues; Buddhist temples; and at least one mosque.

Southwest Houston features development from all decades, with older neighborhoods dating back to the late 1950s and early 1960s and newer residential development that continues today. The area's large geographical coverage makes for varying landscapes and neighborhoods of differing characteristics. Almost any type of housing—including blocks of inexpensive, low-rise apartment complexes, modest single-family residential homes, large elegant residences, townhomes, and mansions—can be found here.

MEYERLAND

Meyerland was established in the 1950s by George Meyer, whose family owned the area just south of Bellaire, along Brays Bayou. It quickly became associated with Houston's post–World War II Jewish community. Several institutions, such as the Jewish Community Center, Congregation Beth Israel, Congregation Beth Yeshurun, and a few smaller synagogues, are located here. The greenbelt along Brays Bayou is a popular place for residents to jog, walk, and bike. Graced by moss-covered oaks, its scenic route meanders through the neighborhood.

Homes here include older one-story bungalows, ranch houses, and more recent brick structures. They range from $150,000 to more than $500,000 but are generally more affordable than those inside the 610 Loop. In addition, most of the residents are zoned to Bellaire High School but do not have to pay Bellaire property tax rates or home prices. Meyerland is next to the Inner Loop neighborhood of Stella Link/Linkwood and the City of Bellaire. Because of its location along the bayou, flooding has been a problem at times. Brays Bayou is deep, and it takes quite a bit of rain for it to overflow. The city's growth, along with severe weather, however, have made flooding a bigger issue. Another factor contributing to the

Meyerland

flooding is the fact that the area that is now Meyerland was once a rice field and is in a low-lying area.

Websites: www.houstontx.gov, www.meyerlandonline.com
Area Code: 713
Zip Code: 77096
Post Office: South Post Oak Station, 5505 Belrose Dr, Bldg A, Houston
Police Precincts: Houston Police Department: Fondren Patrol, 11168 Fondren Rd, 713-773-7900; Southwest Patrol, 4503 Beechnut St, 713-314-3900
Emergency Hospitals: Twelve Oaks Hospital, 4200 Portsmouth St, 713-623-2500; Texas Medical Center, www.tmc.edu: Hermann Hospital, www.memorialhermann.org, 6411 Fannin St, 713-704-4000; Ben Taub, www.hchdonline.com, Ben Taub General Hospital, 1504 Taub Loop, 713-873-2000; Methodist Hospital, www.methodisthealth.com, 6565 Fannin St, 713-790-3311; VA Hospital, www.houston.med.va.gov, 2002 Holcombe Blvd, 1-800-553-2278; St. Luke's, www.sleh.com, 6720 Bertner Ave, 832-355-1000; Texas Children's Hospital, www.texaschildrenshospital.org, 6621 Fannin St, 832-824-1000
Libraries: Houston Public Library, www.hpl.lib.tx.us: Meyer Branch, 5005 W Bellfort St, 832-393-1840; McGovern–Stella Link Branch, 7405 Stella Link Rd, 832-393-2630
Adult Education: Houston Community College, West Loop Center, 5601 W Loop S Fwy, 713-718-7868
Public Education: Houston Independent School District, www.houstonisd.org, 4400 W 18th St, Houston, 713-556-6005
Community Publications: *Houston Chronicle*, www.chron.com; *Houston Press*, www.houstonpress.com
Community Resources: City Hall, 900 Bagby St, Houston, 713-837-0311; Jewish Community Center, www.jcchouston.org, 5601 S Braeswood Blvd, Houston, 713-729-3200; YMCA Weekley Family Branch, www.ymcahouston.org, 7101 Stella Link Rd, Houston, 713-664-9622; Southwest Houston Chamber of Commerce, www.gswhcc.org, 6900 S Rice Ave, Bellaire, 713-666-1521
Public Transportation: Harris County Metropolitan Authority, www.ridemetro.org: *Bus*: 10, 33, 47, 49, 65, 68, 261

WESTBURY

Located just outside Loop 610, Westbury is conveniently near the Medical Center, the Galleria/Uptown area, and Reliant football stadium, and offers easy access to downtown Houston. In addition, many of the sprawling ranch-style homes are relatively affordable at around $120,000 to $200,000. As housing prices have increased inside the Loop, many are looking to Westbury as an alternative market. The closer you are to Loop 610, the nicer the residential areas. As you move away from Loop 610, toward South Gessner, the quality of the neighborhood starts to decline.

Westbury

Westbury was developed in the 1950s and 1960s as a suburban community. Eventually annexed by Houston as the city grew, it is no longer considered part of the suburbs. When the real estate market crashed in the 1980s, many area businesses closed. Homes here are typically sprawling one-story ranch-style houses with low-slung roofs and large front and back yards on quiet residential streets. You'll also find many low-rise apartment complexes, mainly around the Westbury Square shopping center.

Greater Fondren Southwest Area

Bounded by Braeswood on the north, Fondren on the east, West Airport on the south, and Gessner on the west, this area was largely undeveloped until the 1970s, when developers built large fancy homes on the pristine land here. Fondren Southwest homes were highly sought after by prospective buyers. Secluded behind a brick wall, Fondren Southwest had the feel of a special neighborhood. These days, the neighborhood is less special. A maze of apartment complexes was built in the empty lots around it in the 1970s and 1980s. After the housing slump in the 1980 the area deteriorated. Struggling to find people to occupy the complexes, landlords decreased rent prices and rented to anyone regardless of criminal background or character. Though the Fondren Southwest homes behind the brick barrier are generally safe and isolated from the surrounding apartments, the apartment complexes around them have very high crime rates.

Glenshire

Farther south of Fondren Southwest, behind West Bellfort, lies the hidden neighborhood of Glenshire. Tall trees that form a canopy line the neighborhood's main entrance. This well-kept secret contains affordable homes of varying sizes and

HOUSTON: SOUTHWEST HOUSTON

styles. The variety of designs is a departure from the uniform-looking brick homes that populate most of the newer residential neighborhoods. Here you'll find Old English style Tudor homes, traditional, Tidewater-style, and other designs. **East Glenshire** homes are larger and have lovely landscaped lawns and yards. **West Glenshire** homes are smaller and feature some townhomes. Outside of East Glenshire is a recently constructed neighborhood named **Villages of Glenshire**, which has smaller one- and two-story brick homes with minimal lots.

Website: www.houstontx.gov
Area Code: 713
Zip Codes: 77031, 77071, 77035, 77096
Post Offices: South Post Oak Station, 5505 Belrose Dr, Bldg A; Westbury Station, 11805 Chimney Rock Rd; Westbrae Station, 10910 S Gessner Dr
Police Precincts: Houston Police Department: Fondren Patrol, 11168 Fondren Rd; Southwest Patrol, 4503 Beechnut St, 713-314-3900; Westbury Storefront, 5550 Gasmer Dr, 713-728-2424
Emergency Hospitals: Memorial Hermann Southwest Hospital, www.memorialhermann.org, 7600 Beechnut St; Texas Medical Center, www.tmc.edu: Hermann Hospital, www.memorialhermann.org, 6411 Fannin St, 713-704-4000; Ben Taub, www.hchdonline.com, Ben Taub General Hospital, 1504 Taub Loop, 713-873-2000; Methodist Hospital, www.methodisthealth.com, 6565 Fannin St, 713-790-3311; VA Hospital, www.houston.med.va.gov, 2002 Holcombe Blvd, 800-553-2278; St. Luke's, www.sleh.com, 6720 Bertner Ave, 832-355-1000; Texas Children's Hospital, www.texaschildrenshospital.org, 6621 Fannin St, 832-824-1000
Libraries: Houston Public Library, www.hpl.lib.tx.us: Meyer Branch, 5005 W Bellfort St, 832-393-1840; Morris Frank Branch, 6440 W Bellfort, 832-393-2410
Adult Education: Houston Community College, West Loop Center, 5601 W Loop S Fwy, 713-718-7868
Public Education: Houston Independent School District, www.houstonisd.org, 4400 W 18th St, 713-556-6005
Community Publications: *Houston Chronicle*, www.chron.com; *Houston Press*, www.houstonpress.com
Community Resources: City Hall, 900 Bagby St, Houston, 713-837-0311, Southwest Houston Chamber of Commerce, www.gswhcc.org, 6900 S Rice Ave, Bellaire, 713-666-1521; Westbury Civic Club, www.westburycrier.com, 713-723-5437; Marian Community Center, 11101 S Gessner Dr, Houston, 713-773-7015
Public Transportation: Harris County Metropolitan Authority, www.ridemetro.org: *Bus:* 8, 10, 46, 47, 65, 68, 163, 262, 265, 292

WESTWOOD/HARWIN, SHARPSTOWN, AND ALIEF

Westwood/Harwin

Westwood is a working-class, lower-income neighborhood, primarily consisting of low-rise apartments and commercial areas. There are a few townhomes and small homes here, but low-rent apartments predominate in this neighborhood. The **Harwin** area is named after a street known throughout Houston as the place to buy counterfeit goods. Nearby on Hillcroft are several Persian, Indian, and Pakistani restaurants, grocery stores, and clothing stores. This is the city's South Asian commercial center, and many recent immigrants from South Asian countries live in the apartments off Bellaire Boulevard, on the other side of US 59 across from Sharpstown Mall. A large white mosque stands out in this quiet residential area that is surrounded by a few commercial businesses. Most of the city's South Asian and Middle Eastern residents, however, do not reside here but are instead spread throughout Houston.

Braeburn

Those interested in the Sharpstown or Fondren Southwest area might consider the small neighborhood of Braeburn. Bounded by Bissonnet on the north, Hillcroft on the east, Brays Bayou on the south, and US 59 on the west, Braeburn is located between Sharpstown and Fondren Southwest. It features mostly single-story homes on tidy but lush, well-maintained lawns on quiet residential streets.

Sharpstown

At the time of its development in the late 1950s and early 1960s, Sharpstown was a groundbreaking community. It was the largest suburb in Texas with the first indoor air-conditioned mall. Young families flocked to this new, promising community with tidy homes on neatly divided lots, wide streets, convenient shopping, and new schools. From the 1960s to early 1970s this was Houston's premier suburb. The success of communities like Sharpstown jump-started the development of similar communities. Sharpstown's sprawling suburban model was adopted many times over and continues to be used in new residential developments. Sharpstown, however, started to steadily decline in the 1980s, when oil prices fell and many workers were laid off, causing the banks to foreclose on their homes. The decline was also due in part to white flight and the attraction of newer suburbs. Though Sharpstown has never recovered its former glory, there is no shortage of buyers interested in the homes here. It has an excellent location near US 59 and major arteries such as Bellaire Boulevard. The community lies between the Inner Loop and the suburbs.

Recent immigrants from Asia and Latin America have taken the place of former residents, making Sharpstown one of the most diverse neighborhoods in

Sharpstown

Houston. All along Bellaire Boulevard between US 59 and Beltway 8, drivers can see shop signs in English, Spanish, Chinese, and Vietnamese. Stores that cater to the Hispanic population's tastes have replaced many of the stores that closed and relocated to other areas. The Safeway is now a Fiesta grocery store and instead of Winchell's Donuts, there are taco stands and Mexican bakeries. On some streets like Beechnut, neighborhood Hispanic mercados fill the gap for residents who need daily necessities but have no transportation.

The city's Chinatown and Vietnamese commercial centers are located here and have replaced open land. Houston actually has two Chinatowns. The original one is downtown, but most are familiar only with the one located in Sharpstown. It is more of a commercial district with shops, grocery stores, restaurants, banks, and other businesses than a residential area. Chinatown starts in Sharpstown on Bellaire Blvd and extends past Beltway 8 into the Alief community. Visitors will find some of the city's best Chinese restaurants and bakeries and plenty of bubble tea here. Most of the signs are in Chinese, and you really get the feeling that you've stepped into another zone, even possibly a foreign land. Over the years, however, Sharpstown slowly has developed into a residential community as well. Many new immigrants live in the apartments behind Bellaire Boulevard, which allows them to be within walking distance of area amenities. In addition, senior citizen apartments are being constructed in the middle of an area with several shops, creating a pedestrian village. On the other side of Bellaire Boulevard, hidden behind the busy thoroughfare, is a single-family residential neighborhood. Homes vary in size and style and are relatively affordable.

Because Sharpstown covers such a large area, the housing here is diverse and varies from neighborhood to neighborhood. Sharpstown's only high-rise condominium, the Conquistador, is located across from Sharpstown Mall. The area around Houston Baptist University, along the feeder of US 59 at Fondren, is a series of strip shopping centers, university dorms, and single-family residential homes off the street. One of the biggest employers in the area, Hermann Memorial

Hospital Southwest, is located near the university, and many of its employees live in Sharpstown and its surrounding areas. Beechnut Street contains many low-rise apartment complexes and duplexes, mostly rented by Mexican and Latin American immigrants. The single-family residential homes hidden behind this street are similar in style and price to those behind Bellaire Boulevard. Behind Sharpstown High School are homes on large lots that are secluded behind trees.

Sharpstown further declined in the 1990s as residents and businesses began moving farther out to newer suburbs. Some of the boarded-up buildings in strip shopping centers along Gessner and Beechnut make the area look like a deserted ghost town. The many car dealerships that once stood on Bellaire Boulevard have all moved farther down US 59 near the new suburbs in Sugar Land, leaving empty deserted lots or open land. Don't let the appearance of the major thoroughfares fool you, however. Once you deviate from the main roads onto the residential streets, you'll find nice residential neighborhoods with homes that have large lawns.

Sharpstown has a bad reputation as a shady part of town, and indeed parts of it are considered high-crime areas. The crimes are mostly concentrated near Sharpstown's numerous low-rise apartments. The community itself is too large to fit into this general stereotype, though. The 1950s-style ranch homes and bungalows still attract many buyers to this diverse community with a balanced mix of African-Americans, Caucasian, Hispanics, and Asians.

Alief

Like Sharpstown, Alief has seen better days. The difference between the two is that parts of Alief, mainly the western portions, have bounced back from the housing slump of the 1980s. During the 1970s and 1980s Alief was a popular residential suburb. At the time it was one of the newest developments and attracted many families with its affordable housing and amenities. The community's high-quality schools also drew in many new residents. The local high school was one of the largest in the state and eventually had to be divided into two.

Alief is a bustling microcosm of nearly every demographic you'll find in Houston. In fact, you'll find globe sculptures at major intersections, inscribed with "ID" which stands for "International District." Over its 30-year boom period, the Alief Independent School District (AISD), formed in 1917 and currently supporting 41 campuses, gained national attention in the 1980s for becoming one of the first in the United States to be equally populated by the four major ethnicities: African-American, white, Asian, and Hispanic. The AISD Communications Office reports that more than 80 languages and dialects are spoken among its 45,000 enrolled students.

The downturn in the real estate market following the oil bust in the 1980s changed Alief. Many homeowners faced foreclosure. New home construction stopped but picked up again during the economic boom of the 1990s. Most of the new residential construction is farther west, near the Fort Bend County line. New homes, however, mix with older homes in some of the old neighborhoods.

Alief

The area closer to Sharpstown is glum, with row after row of strip shopping centers lining the major thoroughfares. There are also many auto repair shops and light industries in the eastern part of Alief near Beltway 8. Farther down the street, past Beltway 8 into Alief, is a continuation of Chinatown, though the businesses here are primarily Vietnamese. Just 15 years ago this area was largely flat open land. KBR (Halliburton) was one of the few businesses here, and the Beltway had been completed just a few years earlier.

Housing in Alief includes townhomes and small one-story homes dating from the 1970s. Farther west, toward the newly constructed Westpark Tollway, you'll find a mix of new and established residential developments. Homes here are surrounded by lush vegetation and other lovely flowers planted by the owners. The neighborhoods here are quieter than in eastern Alief and more compatible with the description of a residential community because of the absence of commercial businesses, such as the light industries in east Alief.

Many now consider Alief to be part of Houston, but it's also a community with a separate and independent identity. Its history dates back to 1861, when the first settlers moved in. Back then the town was known as Dairy or Dairy Station, but the name was changed to Alief in 1895 in honor of the town's first postmistress, Alief Ozella Magee. This rural community grew primarily corn, cotton, and rice, and raised cattle. By the 1970s most of Alief was annexed by Houston. According to Alief.com, the population quadrupled between 1970 and 1985. By the 1980s, Houston had annexed all of it except for a tiny township of a few blocks. The opening of the Westpark Tollway provides a quick and direct route for commuters in the outer Alief neighborhoods to inside the Loop and downtown.

The outlying master-planned community of **Mission Bend**, which straddles Harris and Fort Bend counties, lies at the outermost edge of Alief. The community consists of seemingly identical brick single-family residential homes and strip malls.

Website: www.houstontx.gov

Area Code: 713

Zip Codes: 77036, 77074, 77072, 77081, 77083, 77082, 77099

Post Offices: De Moss Branch, 6500 De Moss Dr; Beechnut Station, 11703 Beechnut St; Alief Station, 11936 Bellaire Blvd, Alief; Rich Hill Station, 2950 Unity Dr; Ashford West Station, 12655 Whittington Dr

Police Precincts: Houston Police Department: Southwest Patrol, 4503 Beechnut St, 713-314-3900; Ranchester Storefront, 9146 Bellaire Blvd, 713-272-3673; Westwood Storefront, 9700 Bissonnet St, Ste #1740-W, 713-773-7000

Emergency Hospital: Memorial Hermann Southwest Hospital, www.memorialhermann.org, 7600 Beechnut St, 713-456-5000

Libraries: Houston Public Library, www.hpl.lib.tx.us: Walter Branch Library, 7660 Clarewood Dr, 832-393-2500; Henington-Alief Branch, 7979 South Kirkwood Rd, 832-393-1820

Adult Education: Houston Baptist University, www.hbu.edu, 7502 Fondren Rd, 281-649-3000; Houston Community College, Alief Center, 13803 Bissonnet St, 713-718-6870

Public Education: Houston Independent School District, www.houstonisd.org, 4400 W 18th St Houston, 713-556-6005; Alief Independent School District, www.aliefisd.net, 12302 High Star Dr, Houston, 281-498-8110

Community Publications: *Houston Chronicle*, www.chron.com; *Houston Press*, www.houstonpress.com

Community Resources: City Hall, 900 Bagby St, 713-837-0311; Southwest Houston Chamber of Commerce, www.gswhcc.org, 6900 S Rice Ave, Bellaire, 713-666-1521; Burnett Bayland Park Community Center, 6200 Chimney Rock Rd, 713-668-4516; Sharpstown Community Center, 6600 Harbor Town Dr, 713-988-5328; Lansdale Community Center, 8201 Roos Rd, 713-272-3687; Houston Chinese Community Center, www.ccchouston.org, 9800 Town Park Dr, 713-271-6100; Alief Community Center, 11903 Bellaire Blvd, 281-564-8130

Public Transportation: Harris County Metropolitan Transit Authority, www.ridemetro.org: *Bus:* 2, 4, 19, 25, 46, 47, 65, 67, 68, 82, 132, 163, 262, 265, 274, 292

SOUTHWEST SUBURBS

FORT BEND COUNTY

One of the fastest growing counties in Texas, Fort Bend County has one of the region's most diverse populations: 57 percent white, 20 percent African-American, 11 percent Asian, and 12 percent Hispanic. Over the past 15 to 20 years, this once agricultural county has experienced explosive growth due to the development of new residential communities. In the northeastern part of the county, where most of the population and businesses are concentrated—Sugar Land, Missouri City,

Stafford, and Meadows Place—new housing development has stretched as far out as Richmond, the county seat.

Website: www.fortbendcounty.org/fort_bend_life/city_profiles.htm

MEADOWS PLACE AND STAFFORD
Meadows Place

As you travel from US 59 north, Meadows Place will be the first incorporated city you approach in Fort Bend County. Residents who commute from here to Houston avoid coming home to the rush hour traffic gridlock farther south on US 59 past Highway 6. Meadows Place is a tiny area that consists mostly of a few blocks of homes, with a population of about 7,000. It is primarily a residential community with a small number of commercial businesses within its city limits. A few restaurants, fast food joints, a bank, a Walgreens drugstore, car dealerships, and a Sam's Wholesale Club are located along US 59 within Meadows Place. The relatively limited number of shops is hardly an inconvenience for residents, as several major shopping centers and restaurants are next door in Stafford or within quick driving distance. In fact, it is difficult to tell which establishments are in Meadows and which are in adjoining Stafford since the two cities flow into each other. Homes date from the 1970s, vary in size and variety, and include one-story traditional homes and two-story Tidewater-style homes. Because of its small geographic area, Meadows Place has a small-community feel and residents can easily become acquainted with one another.

Meadows Place

Stafford

Over the past few decades, the small town of Stafford has promoted itself as a business-friendly community. As a result, many stores have opened along US 59, and

GREATER HOUSTON

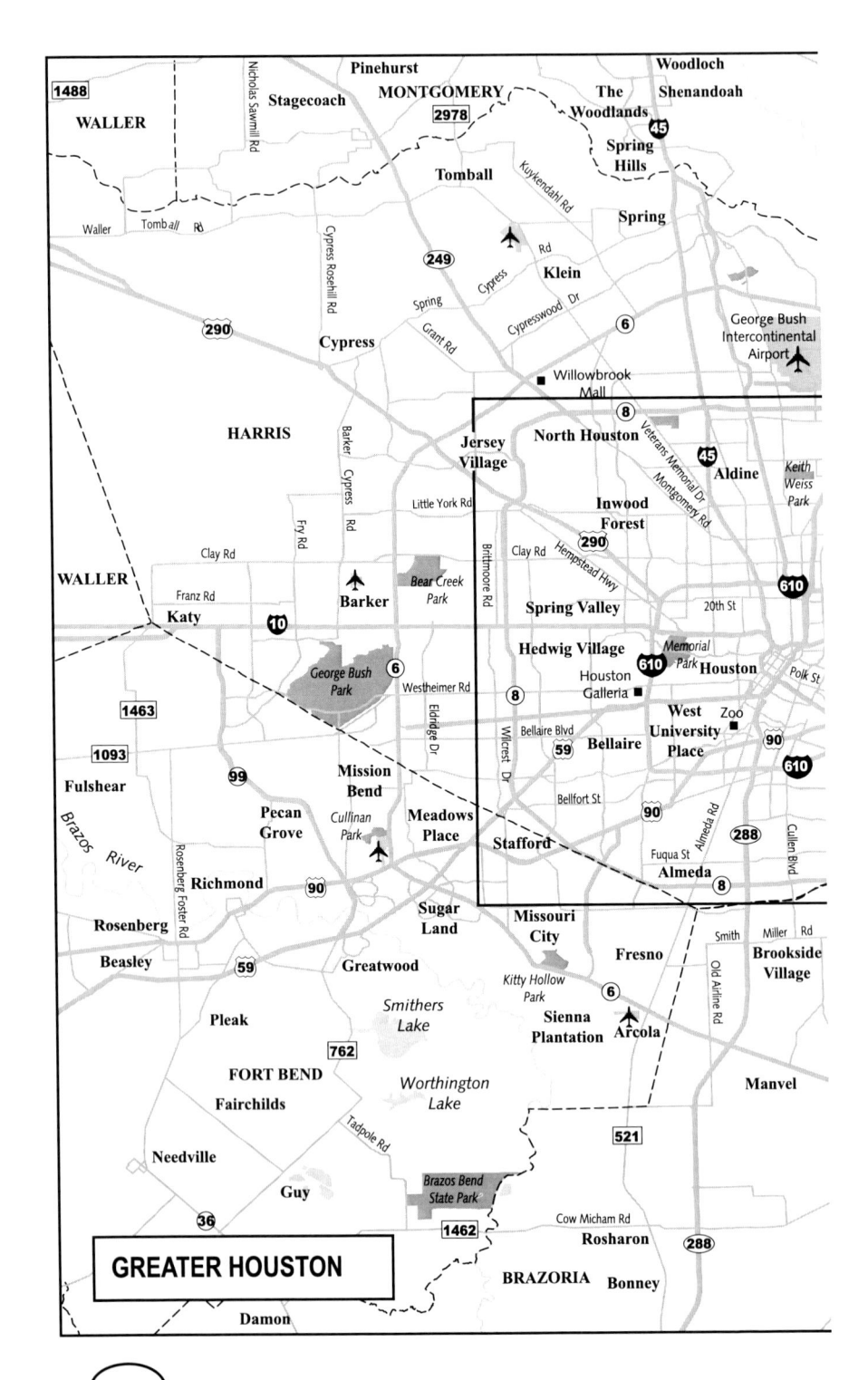

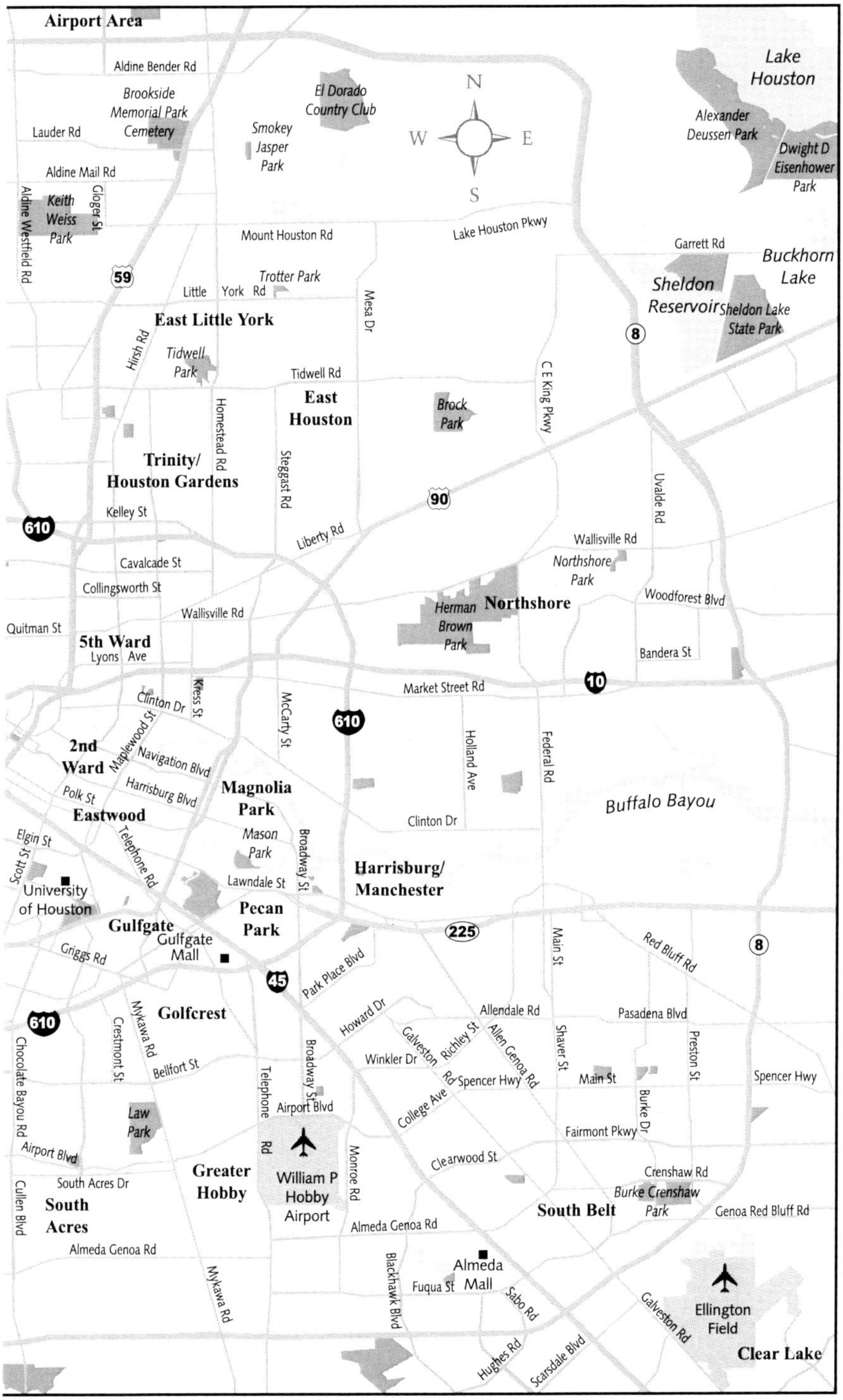
Airport Area
Aldine Bender Rd
Brookside Memorial Park Cemetery
El Dorado Country Club
Lake Houston
Alexander Deussen Park
Dwight D Eisenhower Park
Lauder Rd
Smokey Jasper Park
N
W
E
S
Aldine Mail Rd
Keith Weiss Park
Gloger St
Aldine Westfield Rd
Mount Houston Rd
Lake Houston Pkwy
Garrett Rd
Buckhorn Lake
59
Little York Rd
Trotter Park
Sheldon Reservoir
Sheldon Lake State Park
East Little York
Mesa Dr
8
Hirsh Rd
Tidwell Park
Tidwell Rd
C E King Pkwy
East Houston
Brock Park
Homestead Rd
Trinity/ Houston Gardens
Steggast Rd
Uvalde Rd
90
Kelley St
610
Liberty Rd
Wallisville Rd
Cavalcade St
Northshore Park
Collingsworth St
Woodforest Blvd
Herman Brown Park
Northshore
Wallisville Rd
Quitman St
5th Ward
Lyons Ave
Bandera St
Market Street Rd
10
Clinton Dr
Kress St
McCarty St
610
2nd Ward
Maplewood St
Navigation Blvd
Holland Ave
Federal Rd
Harrisburg Blvd
Magnolia Park
Polk St
Eastwood
Buffalo Bayou
Clinton Dr
Elgin St
Telephone Rd
Mason Park
Broadway St
Scott St
University of Houston
Lawndale St
Harrisburg/ Manchester
Pecan Park
Gulfgate
Gulfgate Mall
225
Main St
Red Bluff Rd
8
Griggs Rd
45
Park Place Blvd
610
Golfcrest
Howard Dr
Allendale Rd
Pasadena Blvd
Mykawa Rd
Crestmont St
Galveston Rd
Richley St
Allen Genoa Rd
Shaver St
Preston St
Chocolate Bayou Rd
Bellfort St
Winkler Dr
Spencer Hwy
Main St
Burke Dr
Spencer Hwy
Telephone Rd
Broadway St
Airport Blvd
College Ave
Law Park
Fairmont Pkwy
Airport Blvd
William P Hobby Airport
Monroe Rd
Clearwood St
Crenshaw Rd
South Acres Dr
Greater Hobby
Burke Crenshaw Park
Cullen Blvd
South Acres
South Belt
Genoa Red Bluff Rd
Almeda Genoa Rd
Almeda Genoa Rd
Blackhawk Blvd
Almeda Mall
Fuqua St
Mykawa Rd
Sabo Rd
Galveston Rd
Ellington Field
Hughes Rd
Scarsdale Blvd
Clear Lake

several companies, including Texas Instruments and UPS, have major offices here. Stafford's lower than average sales tax rate and location between Houston and Sugar Land are the main reasons for its success in attracting revenue-generating businesses. As a result, Stafford's financial position is strong enough that in 1995 it abolished municipal property taxes. Stafford is also unique in that it runs its own school district, the only municipal school district in Texas.

The northern boundaries of the city limits are primarily a commercial area. The glowing signs of restaurants and a few motels border both sides of the freeway until it hits Highway 90. At the intersection of US 59 and Highway 90 are several business parks. In addition, several light industries are located farther inside the city near the railroad tracks.

In the 1820s, William Stafford, Stafford's namesake, settled the town. His was one of the original 300 families that took up Spain's offer of land grants to settle the Texas territory. During the war for Texas's independence from Mexico, Mexican General Santa Anna's troops stopped in the area and survived on the area's food. Farming was the main industry of this town until the 1950s, when light industry and other businesses began to move into the area. All that remains of historic Stafford are a few old buildings of a small farming town that are reminiscent of old Main Street, USA.

It's estimated that more people work in or visit Stafford than actually live here (just under 20,000 residents). You will, however, find a few new single-family residential developments here. Farther inside the city there are also some older bungalow homes with wood siding that date back to the 1950s.

Websites: www.cityofmeadowsplace.org, www.cityofstafford.com
Area Code: 281
Zip Code: 77477
Post Office: Stafford Station, 4110 Bluebonnet Dr, Stafford
Police Departments: Meadows Police Department, One Troyan Dr, Meadows Place, 281-983-2900; Stafford Police Department, www.staffordpd.com, 2702 S Main St, Stafford, 281-261-3950
Emergency Hospitals: Fort Bend Medical Center, www.memorialhermann.org, 3803 FM 1092, Missouri City, 281-499-4800; Methodist Hospital–Sugar Land, www.methodisthealth.com, 16655 Southwest Fwy, Sugar Land, 281-274-7000; Memorial Hermann Southwest Hospital, www.memorialhermann.org, 7600 Beechnut St, Houston, 713-456-5000
Library: Fort Bend County Library, www.fortbend.lib.tx.us: Mamie George Branch, 320 Dulles Ave, Stafford, 281-491-8086
Adult Education: Houston Community College–Stafford, http://swc2.hccs.edu, 9910 Cash Rd, Stafford, 713-718-7800
Public Education: Fort Bend Independent School District (Meadows Place), www.fortbend.k12.tx.us, 16431 Lexington Blvd, Sugar Land, 281-634-1000; Stafford

Municipal School District, www.stafford.msd.esc4.net, 1625 Staffordshire Rd, Stafford, 281-261-9200
Community Publications: *Fort Bend Southwest Star*, www.fortbendstar.com; *Fort Bend Southwest Sun*, www.fortbendsouthwestsun.com
Community Resources: Meadows Place City Hall, One Troyan Dr, Meadows Place, 281-983-2950; Stafford City Hall, 2610 S Main St, Stafford, 281-261-3900; Stafford Centre, www.staffordcentre.com, 10505 Cash Rd, Stafford, 281-208-6900

SUGAR LAND

The City of Sugar Land is named after what was once its main economic export: sugar. The area was at one time a sugar plantation. At the turn of the 20th century, the Imperial Sugar Company headquarters and refinery built Sugar Land, a self-contained company town with its own housing, schools, and hospital. For decades the Imperial Sugar Company was the economic base and major employer of this town. In the past 35 years, however, Sugar Land has evolved from a blue-collar refinery town and agriculturally based economy to a booming, affluent suburb of Houston, with a population approaching 80,000.

This quintessential suburb of master-planned communities—some with their own country clubs, golf courses, and lakes—attracts families from ethnically diverse backgrounds. The city is more than 60 percent white, almost one-quarter Asian, 8 percent Hispanic, and 5 percent African-American. These statistics also reflect the many immigrants from India, China, Taiwan, Russia, and Latin America who have settled in Sugar Land. Like many others who choose Sugar Land, they are drawn by the relatively lower property taxes, the wide selection of single-family residential housing at prices that range from the relatively affordable to millions of dollars, and the well-regarded public school system. Therefore, it comes as no surprise to many that this popular suburb was named by *Money* magazine as one of its top 100 best small cities in 2008.

Being mostly a series of master-planned communities, Sugar Land has an almost uniform look with elegant dark brick buildings, evenly spaced trees, and a town square that includes apartments, condos, the new city hall, shops, hotel, and restaurants all within walking distance of one another. This smartly designed mixed-use area provides the city with a center and sense of community and reflects its shift from an agricultural area to an urban/suburban community.

Though the sugar refinery closed in 2003, its impact on the local economy was minimal. The city has attracted major companies such as Schlumberger, Fluor, and Unocal, which provide employment to residents.

Sugar Land consists of several large subdivisions and communities. The most recognizable is **First Colony**. Sugar Land's City Hall, shopping, entertainment, and dining establishments are located here at Town Center. First Colony contains a mix of single-family residential homes, apartments, lofts, and townhomes. Other subdivisions in Sugar Land include **Sugar Creek**, **Settlers Way/Settlers Park/Settlers Grove**, **New Territory**, **Greatwood**, and **Avalon**. Some of these are self-contained communities that feature amenities such as manmade lakes, waterfalls, fountains, and streams, as well as sailing, canoeing, and a recreation center.

Website: www.ci.sugar-land.tx.us
Area Code: 281
Zip Codes: 77478, 77479, 77477
Post Offices: Sugar Land Station, 225 Matlage Way; First Colony Station, 3130 Grants Lake Blvd
Police Department: Sugar Land Police Department, 1200 Hwy 6 S, 281-275-2500
Emergency Hospital: Methodist Hospital–Sugar Land, www.methodisthealth.com, 16655 Southwest Fwy, 281-274-7000
Libraries: Fort Bend County Library, www.fortbend.lib.tx.us: Sugar Land Branch, 550 Eldridge Rd, 281-277-8934; First Colony Branch, 2121 Austin Pkwy, 281-265-4444
Adult Education: University of Houston–Sugar Land Branch, www.uhsa.uh.edu, 14000 University Blvd, 281-275-3300
Public Education: Fort Bend Independent School District, www.fortbend.k12.tx.us, 16431 Lexington Blvd, 281-634-1000
Community Publications: *Fort Bend Southwest Star,* www.fortbendstar.com; *Fort Bend Southwest Sun,* www.fortbendsouthwestsun.com; *Fort Bend Herald; Texas Coaster*
Community Resources: City Hall, 2700 Town Center Blvd N, 281-275-2700; Fort Bend Chamber of Commerce, www.fortbendchamber.org, 445 Commerce Green Blvd, 281-491-0800

MISSOURI CITY

In the 1890s two Houston real estate investors advertised land for sale in northeast Fort Bend/Southwest Harris County, Texas. To attract buyers from up north in St. Louis, Missouri, they called the area in northeast Fort Bend County "Missouri City." Enough residents moved here for the area to develop into a farming and ranching community. It remained an agricultural area until the period between the 1970s and 1980s when its population went from less than 5,000 to more than 20,000. Unlike the surrounding Fort Bend County communities, Missouri City does not have any significant industry or economic base to support it. Most of its residents commute to Houston for work. This bedroom community has one of the area's most diverse populations: 38 percent white, 38 percent African-American, and 11 percent Hispanic. Missouri City's significant African-American middle-class population began to settle here in the 1970s. Homes are available in various price ranges, including one-story brick homes, million-dollar mansions, and gated estates.

Apartments and condominiums, however, are rare to nonexistent because of local zoning ordinances.

A small portion of Missouri City lies within Harris County. The homes closer to the Harris County line are usually older and more affordable. Farther out past Highway 6 are several master-planned communities with homes in various price ranges.

The suburbs of Houston are full of master-planned communities far from the center of the city. In many instances they are not suburbs but isolated communities designed by developers to take advantage of the low land values and scenic natural surroundings. They often attract people who are concerned about crime in the city, are looking for good public schools, and are lured by the idea of being in an area surrounded by nature. Communities such as these include the following:

Oyster Creek

Named for a nearby creek of the same name, Oyster Creek is distinguished by pecan groves, lakes, and golf courses. Nearby is **Quail Valley**, which is located among pecan groves along Oyster Creek.

Lake Olympia

Lake Olympia features waterfront homes, gated communities, and single-family homes from $150,000 into the millions. Residents can enjoy the use of two Olympic-size pools, tennis courts, a private marina, boating and fishing piers, and four parks.

Lake Olympia

Sienna Plantation

Sienna Plantation is on the site of a former sugar cane plantation once owned by Jonathan Waters, a planter from South Carolina. Known at the time as the Waters Plantation, it became a prosperous estate with sugar cane, cotton, and other crops.

The estate includes an impressive mansion that overlooks a pecan grove with a sugar mill and sawmill. After the Civil War, the plantation was sold and changed hands several times before Lillian and Stella Scanlan inherited the property upon the death of their father, former Houston Mayor T.H. Scanlan. The two sisters renamed it Sienna Plantation and converted it to a working ranch. From 1955 to 1967 it was used as a retreat for Catholic nuns. Developers restored the mansion when work began on this residential community.

Sienna Plantation contains a variety of homes that range from $130,000 to more than $2 million. It's located in a scenic and rural area that overlooks the Brazos River. The community's isolation and distance from nearby development provides the kind of quiet, safe atmosphere that makes people willing to put up with a long commute. To compensate, developers have created a resort-style recreation complex known as Club Sienna, with a golf course, private stables, outdoor amphitheater, and outdoor sports park. Club Sienna gives residents the feeling that they are in a park or resort rather than a residential neighborhood.

Websites: www.ci.mocity.tx.us, www.siennaplantation.com, www.lakeolympia.org
Area Code: 281
Zip Codes: 77459, 77479, 77489
Post Offices: Missouri City Annex Station, 3701 Glenn Lakes Lane, Missouri City; Missouri City Station, 1902 Texas Pkwy, Missouri City
Police Departments: Missouri City Public Safety Headquarters, 3849 Cartwright Rd, Missouri City, 281-261-4200; Fort Bend Sheriff's Office, 1410 Ransom Rd, Richmond, 281-341-4700
Emergency Hospital: Memorial Hermann Fort Bend Medical Center, www.memorialhermann.org, 3803 FM 1092, Missouri City, 281-499-4800
Library: Fort Bend County Public Library, www.fortbend.lib.tx.us: Missouri City Branch, 1530 Texas Pkwy, Missouri City, 281-499-4100

Sienna

Public Education: Fort Bend Independent School District, www.fortbend.k12.tx.us, 16431 Lexington Blvd, Sugar Land, 281-634-1000; Houston Independent School District, www.houstonisd.org, 4400 W 18th St, Houston, 713-556-6005 (some portions of Missouri City)
Community Publications: *Fort Bend Southwest Star*, www.fortbendstar.com; *Fort Bend Southwest Sun*, www.fortbendsouthwestsun.com; *Fort Bend Herald*; *Texas Coaster*
Community Resources: City Hall, 1522 Texas Pkwy, Missouri City, 281-261-4260; Fort Bend Chamber of Commerce, www.fortbendchamber.org, 445 Commerce Green Blvd, Sugar Land, 281-491-0800

RICHMOND AND ROSENBERG

Located in the heart of Fort Bend County, along the Brazos River, **Richmond** is steeped in history. It was the first settlement in the county and the first incorporated city of the Republic of Texas. Early residents included prominent figures such as Jane Long, Mirabeau B. Lamar, and Deaf Smith, all of whom helped found the Republic and were instrumental in its early years. Until recently, most of the development in Fort Bend County was confined to Sugar Land, Missouri City, and the areas near Houston. As growth increases, development is expanding into Richmond as well.

One of the largest planned communities here is **Pecan Grove Plantation**. This affluent residential community is located approximately 4 miles northeast of Richmond. Most of the residents commute to work in Houston 26 miles away. It is farther than most of the Fort Bend neighborhoods, but its location is part of the attraction. Developed in the 1970s, Pecan Grove Plantation is built around the private Pecan Grove Country Club and golf course. The community is situated among stately pecan trees, huge oak trees, and wooded areas.

Richmond

Next to Richmond is the city of **Rosenberg**. It developed in 1880 around the Gulf, Colorado, and Santa Fe railroad 3 miles west of the city of Richmond after the railroad was denied access through Richmond. Rosenberg is still primarily an agricultural town. The population, however, has changed from the original Czech, Polish, and German settlers to a mostly Hispanic population today.

There are many more planned communities in Fort Bend County, with new home construction continuing in almost all of them. These developments are scattered and spread out around Fort Bend County. For a complete list of Fort Bend's planned communities, check out the following link: www.fortbendcounty.org/fort_bend_life/documents/PlannedCommunitiesTheirDevelopersNovember2010.pdf

Websites: www.ci.richmond.tx.us, www.ci.rosenberg.tx.us, www.pecangrove.org
Area Code: 281
Zip Codes: 77471, 77469
Post Offices: Rosenberg Station, 2103 Ave G, Rosenberg; Richmond Station, 5560 FM 1640 Rd, Richmond
Police Departments: Richmond Police Department, www.richmondtxpolice.com, 600 Preston St, Richmond, 281-342-2849; Rosenberg Police Department, 2120 4th St, Rosenberg, 832-595-3700; Fort Bend Sheriff's Office, 1410 Ransom Rd, Richmond, 281-341-4700
Emergency Hospital: OakBend Medical Center, www.oakbendmedialcenter.org, 1705 Jackson St, Richmond, 281-341-3000
Libraries: Fort Bend County Public Library, www.fortbend.lib.tx.us: George Memorial Library, 1001 Golfview Dr, Richmond, 281-342-4455; Fort Bend County Law Library, Richmond, 401 Jackson St, Rm 302, Richmond, 281-341-3718
Public Education: Lamar Consolidated School District, www.lcisd.org, 3911 Ave I, Rosenberg, 281-341-3100
Community Publications: *Fort Bend Southwest Sun*, www.fortbendsouthwestsun.com; *Herald-Coaster* (Rosenberg), www.herald-coaster.com; *Fort Bend Now*, www.fortbendnow.com
Community Resources: Richmond City Hall, 402 Morton St, Richmond, 281-342-5456; Rosenberg City Hall, 2110 Fourth St, Rosenberg, 832-595-3400; Fort Bend Chamber of Commerce, www.fortbendchamber.org, 445 Commerce Green Blvd, Sugar Land, 281-491-0800; George Ranch Historical Park, www.georgeranch.org, 10215 FM 762, Richmond, 281-343-0218; Brazos Bend State Park, 21901 FM 762, Needville, 979-553-5101

NORTHWEST HOUSTON

This area of Houston continues to grow due to constant construction of new residential developments that attract buyers with affordable options, a quiet lifestyle, and beautiful natural surroundings. Northwest Houston is a heavily treed area surrounded by lush vegetation. Until the 1950s it was primarily a rural area comprised of German farming communities that dated back to the mid 1800s. Serious development of the northwest countryside first started in the 1960s when it was announced that an international airport would be constructed north of the city. Though residential communities had been in the northwest area, development really took off in the late 1980s and early 1990s when the Sam Houston Tollway and improvements to other local highways (Highway 6, FM 1960, and Highway 290) made the area more easily accessible to prospective homeowners.

Many major companies are located here, which also has spurred the growth of its communities. The area's largest employers are Sysco, Hewlett Packard, Baker Hughes, Continental Airlines, and Cooper Industries. In addition, many retail stores and services, most of which are along the heavily traveled FM 1960 (much of which was renamed Cypress Creek Parkway in 2010), provide additional jobs. The opening of major malls in the 1980s and 1990s also has created employment in the area.

INWOOD FOREST, CANDLELIGHT, GARDEN OAKS, AND OAK FOREST

Inwood Forest

One of the first neighborhoods in northwest Houston, Inwood Forest dates back to the late 1960s and early 1970s. Consequently, you may be able to find homes here in the low $100,000s. Houses vary in size from small ranch-style designs to large upscale residences. The major feature of this neighborhood is the renovated private Inwood Forest Golf Club. Inwood Forest has a diverse ethnic population of young families, retiree communities, and professionals. The neighborhood has lost the luster that once was associated with Inwood Forest since the construction of low-income

Inwood Forest

apartment complexes. Those who are simply looking for a nice house near major freeways on the northwest side of town, however, will find a good bargain here.

Candlelight

Quietly secluded among winding roads and a forest of towering trees, Candlelight is a hidden gem. It was developed in the 1970s and remained in an out-of-the-way location until West Tidwell was extended through the neighborhood in the late 1980s. The greenbelts along Cole Creek and White Oak Bayou provide recreational space for walking, biking, and other outdoor activities. Candlelight is divided into the subdivisions of **Candlelight Estates, Candlelight Oaks, Candlelight Forest, Candlelight Place, Candlelight Plaza,** and **Candlelight Woods**. The homes here vary in size and design and cost more than those in surrounding neighborhoods.

Garden Oaks and Oak Forest

The name **Garden Oaks** is appropriate for an area surrounded by lovely gardens, tall pine trees, magnolias, and other vegetation. Development of this neighborhood began in 1937 with several sections added up until the 1950s. For many decades its population was predominantly Catholic working-class families of mostly Polish and Italian backgrounds. The homes here are generally one-story bungalows and ranch-style houses with cedar siding and large well-landscaped lawns that were built for returning World War II vets. Other sections of the neighborhood have larger plantation, ranch, and traditional homes. Because of its location near downtown, Loop 610, and Highway 290, the secret is out about Garden Oaks. It is increasingly becoming a much-sought-after place to live and the site of a great deal of revitalization and redevelopment. The neighborhood has attracted many young couples looking for an affordable home near the city center that they can fix up or add onto. Nearby neighborhoods include **Shepherd Park**, which is bounded by West Tidwell Road on the north, North Shepherd Drive on the east, West 43rd on the south, and Ella Boulevard on the west.

Located south of the Candlelight neighborhood and west of Garden Oaks, **Oak Forest** is another neighborhood with similar natural surroundings. Development began in 1946 in a rural area surrounded by tall pine trees, and the City of Houston annexed Oak Forest in 1949. At the time it was the area's largest suburban neighborhood. Most of the original bungalows were built for returning GIs. Many commercial businesses are located on West 43rd Street and Ella Boulevard. Buyers who have been pushed out of the Garden Oaks housing market because of rising prices due to increasing demand often find Oak Forest a more affordable option. It has the same convenient location and city center near Loop 610 as Garden Oaks.

Websites: www.houstontx.gov, www.candlelightoaks.org, www.gardenoaks.org, www.ofha.org

HOUSTON: NORTHWEST HOUSTON

Area Code: 713
Zip Codes: 77018, 77091, 77092
Post Offices: Garden Oaks Station, 3816 N Shepherd Dr; Oak Forest Station, 2499 Judiway St; Irvington Station, 7825 Fulton St
Police Precincts: Houston Police Department: Northwest Patrol, 6000 Teague Rd, 713-744-0900; Near North Storefront, 1335 W 43rd St, 713-956-3140
Emergency Hospitals: Memorial Hospital Northwest, 1635 N Loop W Fwy, 713-867-2000; LBJ Hospital, 5656 Kelley St, 713-636-5000
Libraries: Houston Public Library, www.hpl.lib.tx.us: Oak Forest Branch, 1349 W 43rd St, 832-393-1960; Collier Regional Branch Library, 6200 Pinemont Dr, 832-393-1740
Public Education: Houston Independent School District, www.houstonisd.org, 4400 W 18th St, 713-556-6005
Community Publications: *Houston Chronicle*, www.chron.com, *Houston Press*, www.houstonpress.com
Community Resources: Antoine Health Center, 5668 W Little York Rd, 281-447-2800; Northside Clinic, 8523 Arkansas St, 713-696-5900; Northwest Health Center, 1100 W 34th St, 713-861-3939; Candlelight Community Center Parks, 1520 Candlelight Lane, 713-682-3587
Public Transportation: Harris County Metropolitan Authority, www.ridemetro.org, *Bus:* 8, 9, 23, 40, 44, 45, 50, 64, 79

CYPRESS AREA

Cypress

Cypress was settled in the 1840s by German immigrants who joined the few ranchers and farmers who were already in the area. It remained an agricultural community, with primarily rice and dairy farming, until the 1950s when suburban development began to encroach upon this community. By the 1980s the surrounding area was a major Houston suburb that included many subdivisions and neighborhoods. According to the 2010 US Census, the Cypress-Fairbanks area grew nearly 70 percent from 2000 to 2010, with a total of 587,142 individuals living in the 10 zip codes within the Cy-Fair Independent School District. The actual community of Cypress was never incorporated. One notable building, Tin Hall, built in the 1880s, still stands. It is reportedly Texas's oldest reception hall and is still in operation.

Located 20 miles from downtown Houston along US Highway 290, the neighborhoods in Cypress are surrounded by large trees. Unlike its cosmopolitan neighbor, Houston, Cypress is more country-western in character. Although Cypress was a rural area decades ago, the continual construction of new homes has taken over the countryside. Many people are attracted by the relatively affordable homes, safe family-oriented neighborhoods, and good public schools.

Jersey Village

Within the Cypress area is the incorporated city of Jersey Village, located in far northwest Houston on the former F&M dairy ranch. The F&M dairy was not only a working farm but also an agricultural entertainment enterprise that allowed the public to watch cows being milked, buy ice cream made from the milk, ride ponies, and enjoy musical entertainment. In 1954 the farm's owner, Clark W. Henry, sold it for residential development. The new community was named for the Jersey dairy cattle that once populated the area. It was incorporated in 1956 and remains an independently governed community.

Jersey Village is no longer the countryside. Suburban sprawl has filled in many of the surrounding areas between Jersey Village and Houston. Most of the commercial development is concentrated along US Highway 290. Despite its suburbanization, Jersey Village still has a quiet, rural atmosphere. The area is very green and filled with many mature trees and other flora. This community primarily attracts families looking for quality schools and a quiet neighborhood in which to raise their kids. Jersey Village has a mix of single-family residential homes that start in the $100,000 range, as well as townhomes and patio homes. Though single-family residential homes predominate, lofts recently have been added to the housing options.

Jersey Village

Klein

Situated halfway between Tomball and Spring, the unincorporated community of Klein has a strong German influence. Evidence of its German heritage is noticeable in local family surnames, including Wunderlich, Hassler, Doerre, and Schindewolf. The community is named in honor of Adam Klein, who established the area's first post office station, which the US Government named after him. He and his wife Friederika, natives of Stuttgart, Germany, along with several other German immigrant families, settled the area by Cypress Creek in the 1840s. They established an agricultural community that they called Big Cypress. It included a Lutheran church, post office, and drugstore. Many of the settlers' early descendants still reside here. Country singer Lyle Lovett, who grew up in Klein, is a direct descendant of Adam Klein.

This formerly quiet, agricultural community is now a growing Houston suburb. Yet it still has a country atmosphere and rural landscape that attract many homebuyers. Tall pine trees, wooded lots, and green spaces are characteristic of neighborhoods here. Klein Independent School District's high-quality public schools are a further draw.

Champion Forest

Living in Champion Forest is like having your own country estate. Grand homes sit on large wooded lots with towering leafy trees. The originally built magnificent residences are unique in design and are a departure from the uniform brick-style homes that characterize most of the newer sections. Though Champion Forest is known for its magnificent mansions and residences, you'll also find more modest homes here.

Located 23 miles from downtown Houston and along the busy, cluttered FM 1960 corridor (recently renamed Cypress Creek Parkway), Champion Forest still has a secluded country atmosphere. Daily conveniences and amenities are a quick drive from Champion Forest. Additionally, Highway US 290, I-45, and the Sam Houston and Hardy Tollways are nearby and offer easy access to other parts of Houston. Nearby attractions include adjacent Raveneaux Country Club. Residents are likely to see many migratory birds, as the area has been designated an official bird sanctuary. Initial development in the area began in the 1970s on farmland. Nearby are The Woodlands community, Willowbrook Mall, Greenspoint Mall, several golf courses and country clubs, Sam Houston Race Park, and the Aerodrome Ice Skating Complex. Those fortunate enough to live in Champion Forest are part of one of Houston's most prestigious neighborhoods. Splendid homes and beautiful natural surroundings are the primary appeal of this neighborhood.

Gleannloch Farms

Developed in the 1950s as a horse farm, Gleannloch Farms was renowned for decades as the premier place for Egyptian Arabian horses. Today it is better known as a master-planned community that features homes from $160,000 to $1,000,000. This very suburban development contains walking and running paths, swimming pools, ponds, recreational lakes, a recreation center, a 27-hole golf course, and an equestrian center. Shopping is minutes away along FM 1960 and nearby Willowbrook Mall.

Gleannloch Farms is divided into neighborhoods by price range. The most expensive homes, which range from $400,000 to $1,000,000, are located in the

Estates subdivision. Homes here sit on large lots in wooded areas. Residents of the Estates have first rights to the stables and horse boarding at the equestrian center.

Copperfield

Copperfield's streets reflect careful consideration of the neighborhood's design and layout. Commercial areas are characterized by uniform-looking buildings and well-maintained streets that are actively enforced by deed restrictions and regulations. Most of the commercial businesses are located on Highway 6.

This master-planned community, developed by the Friendswood Development Corporation, is located just north of the Bear Creek area and approximately 22 miles from downtown Houston. Copperfield is divided into seven subdivisions it calls "villages," each with their own recreational facilities, parks, pools, tennis courts, greenbelts, neighborhood markets, and specialty stores. Residents also can use the community park's picnic facilities, playgrounds, baseball fields, an exercise/running track, a covered pavilion, and a community center. Perhaps one of the most impressive recreational facilities here is the Copperfield Racquet & Health Club, a private club established in 1980 that is open to Copperfield residents. Outside the villages are numerous churches, shopping centers, shops, restaurants, and recreational amenities.

Copperfield

Like many of the master-planned communities in the northwest corridor, Copperfield is near a rural part of the county. It tends to attract families who prefer a quiet place away from the troubles of the city. Although Copperfield was initially developed in 1977, homebuilders continued to construct new, affordably priced homes, custom homes, and townhomes until 2003. Homes are priced from the $80,000s to the $400,000s, with the newer developments located on the east side of Highway 6.

Fairfield

Fairfield is located far away from "civilization" in a semi-rural area along US Highway 290. It is a self-contained community with its own shops, schools, restaurants, entertainment, and other amenities. The community has an athletic club that includes a full-size basketball court, swimming pools, tennis courts, and a 20-acre sports park with a soccer field and baseball diamond. In addition, Fairfield has plenty of parks, neighborhood pools, and greenbelts.

Developed by the Friendswood Development Company, Fairfield continues to grow as it enters its final phase of development. This large master-planned community has enough room for all types of homes, including those on large lots, wooded lots, private culs-de-sac, and lakeside property. Home prices vary greatly depending on size and location.

Websites: www.houstontx.gov, www.visitfairfield.com, www.jerseyvillage.info, www.gleannlochfarms.com, www.copperfield.org
Area Code: 713
Zip Codes: 77040, 77095, 77410, 77429, 77433, 77379, 77069
Post Offices: Cypress Station, 16635 Spring Cypress Rd, Cypress; Fairbanks Station, 7050 Brookhollow W Dr, Houston; Willow Place Station, 12955 Willow Place Dr W, Houston; Cornerstone Station, 14403 Walters Rd, Houston; Klein Station, 7717 Louetta Rd, Spring
Police Precincts: Houston Police Department: Willowbrook Storefront, 12932 Willow Chase Dr, Houston, 281-807-9054, Jersey Village Police Department, 16401 Lakeview Dr, Houston, 713-466-5824; Harris County Sheriff's Office, Northwest Command Station, 23828 FM 249, Tomball, 281-290-2100
Emergency Hospitals: Cypress Fairbanks Medical Center, www.cyfairhospital.com, 10655 Steepletop Dr, Houston, 281-890-4285; Memorial Hospital Northwest, 1635 N Loop W Fwy, Houston, 713-867-2000

Fairfield

Libraries: Harris County Public Library, www.hcpl.net: Cy-Fair College Branch, 9191 Barker-Cypress Rd, Cypress, 281-290-3210; Northwest Branch, 11355 Regency Green Dr, Cypress, 281-890-2665; Barbara Bush at Cypress Creek Branch, 6817 Cypresswood Dr, Spring, 281-376-4610

Adult Education: Cy-Fair College, www.cy-faircollege.com, 9191 Barker Cypress Rd, Cypress, 281-290-3200

Public Education: Cy-Fair Independent School District, www.cfisd.net, 10300 Jones Rd, Houston, 281-897-4000 (serves Cypress, Fairfield, and Copperfield); Klein Independent School District, www.kleinisd.net, 7200 Spring Cypress Rd, Klein, 832-484-7899 (serves Klein, Champion Forest, and Gleannloch Farms)

Community Publication: *Houston Chronicle*, www.chron.com

Community Resources: Bear Creek Park, 3535 War Memorial Dr, Houston, 281-496-2177; Cy-Fair Chamber of Commerce, www.cyfairchamber.org, 11050 FM 1960 W, Ste 100, Houston, 281-955-1100

Public Transportation: Harris County Metropolitan Authority, www.ridemetro.org, *Bus:* 86, 214 (Park and Ride)

TOMBALL

Located partially in far northwest Harris County and partially in Montgomery County, Tomball is a town with a decidedly country twist. Unlike Houston, it prides itself on its small-town country character. Though Tomball is only approximately 30 miles northwest of downtown Houston, it's easy for people to mistake Tomball for a city in another corner of the state when they hear the residents' distinctive twang. The area features tall pine trees, creeks, new developments, and historic buildings. Residents usually do not wander out of the area much because everything they need, including commercial businesses, shopping, restaurants, and entertainment, is located either in Tomball or surrounding communities.

Tomball

Settled in the early 1800s by German and other European settlers, the town soon developed into a small farming community called Peck. In 1907 it was renamed Tomball in honor of Senator Thomas Ball for his work in routing railroads through the town. The trains were instrumental in transporting agricultural produce from the region and contributed to Tomball's prosperity. The area remained an agricultural and ranching community for the next few decades. The discovery of oil in 1933 allowed the Humble Oil Company to negotiate a deal with the city in which residents would receive free gas and water for the next 90 years in exchange for drilling rights within the city.

Those considering moving this far out also might consider the nearby town of **Magnolia**, located minutes away in Montgomery County.

Website: www.ci.tomball.tx.us
Area Codes: 281, 832
Zip Code: 77375
Post Office: Tomball Station, 122 N Holderrieth Blvd, 77375-9998
Police Department: Tomball Police Department, 400 Fannin St, 281-255-3908
Emergency Hospital: Tomball Regional Hospital, www.tomballhospital.org, 605 Holderrieth Blvd, 281-401-7500
Library: Harris County Public Library, www.hcpl.net: Tomball Branch, 30555 Tomball Pkwy, 832-559-4200
Adult Education: Lonestar-Tomball College, www.lonestar.edu/tomball.htm, 30555 Tomball Pkwy, 281-351-3300
Public Education: Tomball Independent School District, www.tomballisd.net, 221 W Main St, Tomball, 281-357-3100
Community Publication: The Tribune, www.tribunenews.com
Community Resource: Tomball Area Chamber of Commerce, www.tomballchamber.org, 14011 Park Dr, Ste 111

NORTH HOUSTON AND SURROUNDING COMMUNITIES

NORTHLINE AND GREENSPOINT

Northline

The Northline area is a lower-middle to low-income neighborhood immediately north of downtown. It contains a mix of residential areas, light industries, and strip retail centers. The residences here are mostly small wood frame homes and low-rise apartment complexes. When development began in the 1960s and 1970s, Northline was an undeveloped area covered by open land and trees. Much has changed since then, and it is now a densely populated area with a diverse population. As with any neighborhood near Loop 610 or downtown, there is talk of redeveloping and revitalizing this area.

Greenspoint

Greenspoint's tall glass office buildings and towers stand out conspicuously among the surrounding flat landscape and low-lying structures. It looks much like the downtown central business district but is actually one of several business districts in the metropolitan area. In fact, this is north Houston's major commercial center. The area contains a concentration of retailers, hotels, office space, and other businesses, as well as light industry. Many of the businesses here are related to or cater to demand generated by the nearby international airport. Named for its location along Greens Bayou, Greenspoint is 14 miles from downtown Houston and near the airport and communities north of Houston. It is ideally situated in the center of major commercial activity. The swift increase in job and population growth in the 1970s led to rapid development of new communities in north Houston. I-45, US 59, and the construction of the Hardy Tollway/Sam Houston Parkway provide easy access into and out of the area and have contributed to its commercial and residential growth.

Before the 1960s the area that is now Greenspoint was a mere travel stop along a major travel route. It originally consisted of undeveloped land with some agricultural activity and a few businesses off the major freeways that serviced people passing through the area. The opening of the Bush Intercontinental Airport during the 1960s created a new local economy that provides many of the area's jobs. New residential development alongside existing ones such as **Champions** and **Imperial Valley** offers many additional subdivisions and apartment complexes. Housing here is very affordable when compared to the Inner Loop and even the northwestern suburbs. It has a reputation as a moderate to low-income area and some parts are considered undesirable. Private investors have made recent efforts to revive rundown sections of Greenspoint and convert them into attractive, new residential developments. One of these projects is **CityView**, a large upscale apartment community with two parks.

Websites: www.greenspoint.org, www.houstontx.gov
Area Code: 713
Zip Codes: 77038, 77060, 77066, 77067
Post Offices: Greens North Station, 1530 Greensmark Dr; Cornerstone Station, 14403 Walters Rd
Police Precinct: Houston Police Department: Greenspoint Storefront, 105 Greenspoint Mall, 281-875-6155
Emergency Hospital: York Plaza Hospital and Medical Center, 2807 Little York Rd, 713-697-7777
Library: Harris County Public Library, www.hcpl.net: Aldine Branch, 11331 Airline Dr, 281-445-5560

Adult Education: Lonestar College-North Harris County Campus, www.lonestar.edu/northharris.htm, 2700 W.W. Thorne Dr, 281-618-5400

Public Education: Aldine Independent School District, www.aldine.k12.tx.us, 14910 Aldine Westfield Rd; Spring Independent School District, www.springisd.org, 16717 Ella Blvd, 281-586-1100

Community Publication: *Houston Chronicle*, www.chron.com

Community Resources: City Hall, 900 Bagby St, 713-837-0311; North Greenspoint Chamber of Commerce, www.nhgcc.org, 15600 JFK Blvd, Ste 150, 281-442-8701

Public Transportation: Metropolitan Transit Authority of Harris County, www.ridemetro.org, *Bus:* 56, 86, 102

ALDINE AND SPRING

Aldine

Aldine is one of those small towns that is both a beneficiary and victim of its proximity to a major city's suburban sprawl. Although Aldine was once an independent community, a small portion is now part of the City of Houston, while the rest remains an unincorporated area within Houston's extraterritorial jurisdiction. In other words, Houston has the right to annex the rest of Aldine. Originally established as a stop along the International–Great Northern Railroad, its population hit 100 in 1925. It wasn't until the 1970s, when north Houston started to develop, that this community grew. Today its population is more than 10,000.

Aldine is primarily a lower-middle-income community. Though the town is racially diverse, the population is mostly Hispanic. Several new residential developments offer housing for less than $200,000. There are also many apartment complexes here. Its location near the Sam Houston Tollway (Beltway) and I-45 north offers residents easy access to downtown Houston and employment centers in north Houston.

Spring

Spring is a former small town with a history that dates back to the 1840s, when German immigrants began to farm here. The town grew considerably after the Houston and Great Northern Railroad began to run through here in 1871. The next great growth was the construction of new suburban communities in the 1970s. Spring is one of the fastest growing communities in the Houston area, and residential neighborhoods continually are being constructed.

Spring has a unique historical district known as **Old Town Spring**. Many of the town's oldest buildings are located here and serve as shops. The district's unique and independently owned retail businesses include several antique shops, restaurants, and museums. It is now a tourist attraction where city dwellers and suburbanites come to shop on the weekends.

The town is surrounded by densely wooded forest, which is part of its allure. Spring is a scenic area with neighborhoods surrounded by natural beauty. Homes vary in price, size, and design. There are also townhomes and apartments here. The variety of housing options, trees, and good public schools contribute to the area's popularity and growth. Residents here work in downtown Houston, The Woodlands, the northwest corridor, and at Intercontinental Airport. Residents who work in downtown Houston can get there by getting on I-45. A much quicker route is the Hardy Tollway, which costs $1.50 at each of the two tollbooths, each way. The Woodlands shopping districts and Mitchell concert pavilion are minutes away.

Websites: www.houstontx.gov, www.oldtownspringtx.com
Area Codes: 713, 281
Zip Codes: 77315, 77039, 77379, 77389, 77391, 77373, 77380, 77381, 77382, 77386, 77388, 77389
Post Offices: North Houston Station, 4600 Aldine Bender Rd, Rm 224, North Houston; Spring Station, 1411 Wunsche Loop, Spring; Panther Creek Station, 10800 Gosling Rd, Spring; The Woodlands Station, 9450 Pinecroft Dr, Spring
Police Precincts: Houston Police Department: North Patrol, 9455 W Montgomery Rd, Houston, 281-405-5300; Aldine Community Storefront, 10966 North Fwy, Houston, 281-272-4784; Harris County Sheriff's Office, Substation I–Northwest, 6831 Cypresswood Dr, Spring, 281-376-2997; Harris County Constable Pct 4: 6831 Cypresswood Dr, Spring, 281-376-3472, www.co.harris.tx.us; Harris County Sheriff's Office: Cypresswood Substation, 6831 Cypresswood Dr, Spring, 281-376-2997; 249 Storefront, 7614 Fallbroook Dr, Houston, 281-537-9492, www.hcso.hctx.net
Emergency Hospital: Memorial Hermann The Woodlands Hospital, www.memorialhermann.org, 9250 Pinecroft Dr, The Woodlands, 281-364-2300
Library: Harris County Public Library**,** www.hcpl.net: Aldine Branch, 11331 Airline Dr, 281-445-5560
Adult Education: Lonestar College, lonestar.edu, 2700 W.W. Thorne Dr, Houston, 281-618-5400
Public Education: Aldine Independent School District, www.aldine.k12.tx.us, 14910 Aldine Westfield Rd, Houston; Klein Independent School District, www.kleinisd.net, 7200 Spring-Cypress Rd, Klein, 832-249-4000; Spring Independent School District, www.springisd.org, 16717 Ella Blvd, Houston, 281-586-1100
Community Publication: *Houston Chronicle*, www.chron.com
Community Resources: City Hall, 900 Bagby St, Houston, 713-837-0311; Spring City Hall, Montgomery County, www.co.montgomery.tx.us
Public Transportation: Metropolitan Transit Authority of Harris County, www.ridemetro.org: *Bus:* 86, 204 Aldine: 83, 205, 206, 257

MONTGOMERY COUNTY
The Woodlands

The name of this master-planned community is a perfect description. Set among heavily wooded piney forests, The Woodlands feels like a country lane straight out of a storybook. Conceived as an isolated residential development far from the city, it has proven a popular community for those seeking a serene place to retreat after work. Many communities in the north/northwest area have a similar concept of incorporating the surrounding natural environment with the community. None, however, has come as close as The Woodlands in achieving such a high level of aesthetic beauty and environmental design. The Woodlands' intentional village-community design has resulted in the area leading the way for reviving pedestrian living—it has 160 miles of paved walking/biking paths that are both scenic and safe. Many residents walk to and from homes, schools, churches, and shopping, without ever needing to venture on to a street.

When it was first developed in 1974, The Woodlands was considered extremely far removed from Houston. In fact, it is approximately a one-hour drive from here to downtown Houston, making it the ideal place for people who work in the city and enjoy its conveniences but prefer a less urban environment. In the 1980s residents had to drive to Spring or other communities half-an-hour away for dining, entertainment, shopping, and even groceries. The only exception was the Cynthia Mitchell Woodlands Pavilion, an outdoor concert venue that hosts performances by big-name acts. Now residents do not even have to leave the Woodlands to enjoy themselves. The pedestrian-oriented Woodlands Town Center and Market Square offer dining and shopping along brick-paved streets. Water taxis ferry people from the town center to the Mitchell concert pavilion along the artificially constructed Woodlands Waterway.

The Woodlands

Not every resident commutes to Houston for work. With the development of north and northwest Harris County, many companies and businesses have moved into The Woodlands area, including Anadarko Petroleum Company, Hewitt and Associates, Hughes Christensen, Maersk Sealand, and Chevron Phillips Chemical Company. In addition, Research Forest houses many biomedical and research companies. The Woodlands has achieved its dream of becoming a self-sustaining community within a forest and is fast becoming a major city.

Homes in this predominantly wealthy community of about 94,000 residents come in a wide price range, and most are on heavily wooded lots. Some of the metropolitan area's most magnificent residences are located here. The Woodlands contains six championship golf courses in its country club, miles of hiking and biking trails, and neighborhood parks.

Shenandoah

Just north of The Woodlands, this upscale community is located approximately 35 miles north of Houston along I-45 in the piney forest. It is in a semi-rural community that includes new subdivisions and country homes on spacious lots or several acres. Development originally began in the 1960s as a suburban development, leading to incorporation as a city in 1974. The growth of The Woodlands and the northern Harris County/Montgomery County area has resulted in increasing commercial development and a growing population.

Websites: www.houstontx.gov, www.thewoodlands.com, www.ci.shenandoah.tx.us

Area Codes: 281, 936

Zip Codes: 77381, 77380

Post Office: The Woodlands Station, 9450 Pinecroft Dr, Spring

Police Precinct: Montgomery County Sheriff's Office, www.mocosheriff.com, South Montgomery County Office, 281-297-6500

Emergency Hospital: Memorial Hermann The Woodlands Hospital, www.memorialhermann.org, 9250 Pinecroft Dr, The Woodlands, 281-364-2300

Libraries: Montgomery County Public Library, www.countylibrary.org: South Regional Library, 2101 Lake Robbins Dr, The Woodlands, 936-442-7727; George and Cynthia Woods Mitchell Library, 8125 Ashlane Way, The Woodlands, 936-442-7728

Adult Education: Lonestar College, http://lonestar.edu, 3232 College Park Dr, The Woodlands, 936-273-7500

Public Education: Conroe Independent School District, www.conroeisd.net, 3205 W Davis St, Conroe, 936-709-7751

Community Publications: *Houston Chronicle*, www.chron.com; www.woodlandsonline.com

Community Resources: Montgomery County, 301 N Thompson St, Ste 210, Conroe, 936-756-0571; South Montgomery County Woodlands Chamber of Commerce, www.woodlandschamber.org, 1400 Woodloch Forest Dr, Ste 300, The Woodlands, 281-367-5777

Public Transportation: Brazos Transit District: The Woodlands Express Park and Ride, Sawdust Rd facility, 701 West Ridge Dr, Spring, 281-363-0882; Research Forest facility, 3900 Marisico Pl, The Woodlands, 936-273-6100

NORTHEAST HOUSTON

HUMBLE

Pronounced "umble," with a silent "h," this town was established in the 1840s as an agricultural community and lumber town. The discovery of an oilfield in 1904 transformed it into a boomtown overnight. The Humble Oil Company moved its headquarters to Houston in 1912 and is known today as Exxon. Because of decreasing production from the field, Humble's population began to decline as quickly as it had expanded. Subsequent boom and bust cycles related to the oil industry continued until after World War II. For many years, the town never grew to more than 3,000 and remained a small, quiet community until the opening of the George Bush Intercontinental Airport. The Humble area currently encompasses the area that surrounds the airport, which is one of the major employers here. Furthermore, the completion of US 59 from Humble to Houston attracted new development and more residents.

For decades, Humble had an image as a blue-collar town centered around the oil industry, transportation, and agriculture. Today it is a thriving community outside of Houston with more than 12,000 residents. The town has a down-to-earth, country feel. Many of Humble's residents work in downtown Houston 20 miles away or in industries related to the airport. Old Humble, the historic section of town, contains many antique shops and artists' studios.

KINGWOOD

This master-planned community was developed in the 1970s as a place where residents could live among the heavily wooded areas of north Houston. The Friendswood Development Company, which built Kingwood, attempted to preserve the tall pines, oaks, and other species of trees that cover 14,000 acres on the shores of Lake Houston. Neighborhoods were built into or around the wooded area, where local wildlife abounds—a wise move because the natural beauty and quiet serenity of the area are two of the reasons people are attracted to Kingwood. Retailers moved here over the decades, creating a self-contained community where everything residents needed was inside Kingwood. In addition, miles of greenbelts and hiking/biking trails, parks, swimming pools, a private boat launch, and an equestrian center provide residents with plenty of recreational activities.

The community is divided into villages—26 at last count—each of which has its own distinct architecture. Homes here range from the low $100,000s to million-dollar residences. They include patio homes, townhomes, golf course communities, and lakeside estates. Kingwood was named after King Ranch, which once owned the land here. In 1995, Houston annexed Kingwood, despite fierce opposition from some residents.

Though Kingwood is 22 miles from Houston, residents easily can get to downtown via US 59, the only major freeway that runs through here. The county's public transportation operates a park-and-ride where residents park their cars at the bus depot for an easy commute to major employment centers in downtown Houston, Greenway Plaza, and Greenspoint. In addition, the international airport is nearby.

ATASCOCITA

Atascocita is named after the Atascosito Road, which was the precursor to the present day FM 1960. "Atascocita" is Spanish for "obstruction" and is thought to have once been the site of a garrison used by the Spanish to defend themselves from the French.

This solidly middle-class community located on FM 1960 is approximately 6 miles east of Humble and 18 miles from downtown Houston. It has continued to grow since development began in the 1970s. This unincorporated community lies in a rural part of the county by Lake Houston. It is known as the site of Tour 18, a golf course that re-creates some of the most celebrated golf holes in the US. Within this same community—named by *US News & World Report* as one of the country's best places to retire—swanky neighborhoods and country clubs are neighbors with a state jail and residential probation program.

Websites: www.houstontx.gov, www.cityofhumble.net, www.kingwoodonline.com, www.atascocita.com
Area Code: 281
Zip Codes: 77325, 77346, 77338, 77339, 77345, 77346, 77396
Post Offices: Kingwood Station, 4025 Feather Lakes Way, Kingwood; Humble Station, 1202 1st St E, Humble; Houston Airport Mail Facility, 19175 Lee Rd, Ste 100, Humble
Police Precincts: Houston Police Department: Kingwood Patrol and Storefront, 3915 Rustic Woods Dr, Kingwood, 281-913-4500; Humble Police Department, www.humblepolice.com, 310 N Bender Ave, Humble, 281-446-7127
Emergency Hospitals: Kingwood Medical Center, www.kingwoodmedical.com, 22999 US 59, Kingwood, 281-348-8000; Northeast Medical Center, www.nemch.org, 18951 Memorial North Dr, Humble, 281-540-7700

Libraries: Harris County Public Library, www.hcpl.net: Octavia Fields Branch Library, 1503 South Houston, Humble, 281-446-3377; Kingwood Branch Library, 4400 Bens View Ln, Kingswood, 281-360-6804; Atascocita Branch Library, 19520 Pinehurst Trail Dr, Atascocita, 281-812-2162

Adult Education: Kingwood College, www.kingwoodcollege.com, 20000 Kingwood Dr, Kingwood, 800-883-7939

Public Education: Humble Independent School District, www.humble.k12.tx.us, 20200 Eastway Village Dr, Humble, 281-641-1000; New Caney Independent School District, www.newcaneyisd.org, 21580 Loop 494, New Caney, 281-577-8600 (serves small parts of Kingwood)

Community Publications: *Kingwood Observer*, www.kingwoodobserver.com; *Houston Chronicle*, www.chron.com

Community Resources: City Hall, 900 Bagby St, Houston, 713-837-0311; Humble Area Chamber of Commerce, www.humbleareachamber.org, 110 W Main St, Humble, 281-446-2128; Kingwood Chamber of Commerce, www.kwcommerce.org, 2825 W Town Center Circle, Kingwood, 281-360-4321

Public Transportation: Metropolitan Transit Authority of Harris County, www.ridemetro.org: Kingwood Park and Ride, 3210 Lake Houston Pkwy, *Bus:* 205; Eastex Park and Ride, 14400 Old Humble Rd, east of Eastex, *Bus:* 83, 205, 206, 257

EAST OF HOUSTON

Communities here may be prone to flooding in the event of a hurricane because this is a lower-lying area than other parts of Houston. As a result, the towns and cities here are part of the hurricane evacuation zone. The website of Greater Houston Transportation and Emergency Center (also known as Transtar), www.houstontranstar.org, provides a map with evacuation routes. Further information on hurricane preparedness can be found at the appropriate municipality's website. In addition, the Texas Governor's Office of Emergency Management has established a 211 hotline that those with special healthcare needs and individuals with no transportation can use to register *in advance* for transportation.

PASADENA, DEER PARK, AND BAYTOWN

Pasadena

Pasadena (population about 150,000) resides at the heart of the metropolitan area's petrochemical refining and shipping industries. Its location east of Houston near the Ship Channel and Port of Houston provides companies here with the logistics and transportation necessary to import materials and export products worldwide. This truly is a gritty blue-collar town. Think *Urban Cowboy* with John Travolta, which was actually partly filmed in Pasadena at the famous Gilley's, which burned down

Pasadena

in 1989. This is the type of place where you'll find oil field workers, construction workers, longshoremen, and other individuals employed in heavy industry.

Most people's first introduction to Pasadena is the unpleasant smell coming from the oil refineries and factories. The residents do not seem to mind, but they're probably used to it. Pasadena wasn't always an industrial town. Before the 1930s the lush, fertile land irrigated by the bayous and Gulf waters produced strawberries, cucumbers, flowers, and numerous other fruits. The town still holds an annual strawberry festival in celebration of its past as a major strawberry-producing center.

Pasadena has an ethnically diverse population, approximately half of which is Hispanic. Its residents are primarily in the middle-lower-income bracket. The town offers a variety of housing options that range in price from less than $100,000 to more than a million. They include apartments, townhomes, modest one-story homes, two-story residences in new residential developments, and million-dollar homes. Housing in Pasadena traditionally has been apartments and small one-story homes, reflective of the lower to middle income salary of its residents. Only in recent years has there been development of new suburban neighborhoods with large brick homes and million-dollar mansions.

Deer Park

Next door to Pasadena and the Houston ship channel, Deer Park is home to 32,000 residents, as well as many major refineries and light industries. Established in 1893 on the site of a former park dedicated to deer, this predominantly single-family residential community offers homes in a range of styles and sizes from small one-story bungalows to two-story brick homes. Home prices are relatively affordable, with most of them below $200,000. Like the rest of the metropolitan area, several new and affordable residential developments have been constructed in recent years. Some larger and more extravagant homes or large residential properties are also available in Deer Park.

HOUSTON: EAST OF HOUSTON

Baytown

Baytown, with a population of about 72,000, is one of the cities in the Houston–Sugar Land–Baytown metropolitan area, a US Census–designated metropolitan area. This highly industrialized city is a major center of oil refining, rubber, chemical, and carbon black plants. In 1917 the Humble Oil and Refining Company (now Exxon Corporation) was the first to establish an oil refinery here and was the largest at the time. In fact, the town was built around the Humble refinery. The company built employee housing, paved the roads, and established utility service and schools. Baytown was finally incorporated in 1947 when it consolidated with two other neighboring towns, Pelly and Goose Creek.

Baytown is located 30 miles east of downtown Houston in southeastern Harris and western Chambers County. As its name indicates, this town is located on Galveston Bay. The Lynchburg Ferry crosses the San Jacinto River and provides free transportation around Baytown. Major attractions include boating spots and the Houston Raceway Park, a stadium that hosts drag racing events. The city has a variety of housing options that include apartments, single-family residential homes, several new subdivisions with affordable homes, mansions, and large custom-built homes. Some of the region's most spectacular homes are located in Baytown.

Websites: www.ci.deer-park.tx.us, www.baytown.org, ci.pasadena.tx.us
Area Codes: 281, 409
Zip Codes: 77502, 77503, 77504, 77505, 77506, 77507, 77520, 77521, 77536, 77590, 77591
Post Offices: Pasadena Station, 1199 Pasadena Blvd, Pasadena; John Foster Station, 1520 Richey St, Pasadena; Bob Harris Station, 102 N Munger St, Pasadena; Delbert Atkinson Station, 6100 Spencer Hwy, Pasadena; Baytown Station, 601 W Baker Rd, Baytown; Station A Baytown, 3508 Market St, Baytown; Deer Park Station, 200 E San Augustine St, Deer Park
Police Departments: Baytown Police Department: Main Station, 3200 N Main St, Baytown, 281-422-8371; Community Services Bureau, 220 W Defee St, Baytown; McLemore Substation, 3530 Market St, Baytown; Pasadena Police Department, 1114 Jeff Ginn Memorial Dr, Pasadena, 713-477-1221; Deer Park Police Department, 1410 Center St, Deer Park, 281-478-2000
Emergency Hospitals: San Jacinto Methodist Center, www.methodisthealth.com/sanjacinto, 4401 Garth Rd, Baytown, 281-420-8600; Bayshore Medical Center, www.bayshoremedical.com, 4000 Spencer Hwy, Pasadena, 713-359-2000; Harris County Hospital District, 925 Shaw Ave, Pasadena, 713-740-8180
Libraries: Pasadena Public Library, 1201 Jeff Ginn Memorial Dr, Pasadena, 713-477-0276; Harris County Public Library, South Houston Branch, www.hcpl.net, 607 Ave A, South Houston, 713-941-2385; Sterling Municipal Library (Baytown), www.sml.lib.tx.us, Mary Elizabeth Wilbanks Ave, Baytown, 281-427-7331; Deer Park Public Library, 3009 Center St, Deer Park, 281-478-7208

Adult Education: San Jacinto College, www.sjcd.cc.tx.us: District Campus, 4624 Fairmont Pkwy, Pasadena, 281-998-6150; Central Campus, 8060 Spencer Hwy, Pasadena, 281-476-1501; Texas Chiropractic College, www.txchiro.edu, 5912 Spencer Hwy, Pasadena, 281-487-1170; Lee College (Baytown), www.lee.edu, main campus at Lee Dr and Gulf St, Baytown, 281-427-5611

Public Education: Pasadena Independent School District, www.pasadenaisd.org, 1515 Cherrybrook Lane, Pasadena, 713-740-0000; Deer Park Independent School District, www.dpisd.org, 203 Ivy, Deer Park (also serves eastern portions of Pasadena); La Porte Independent School District, www.laporte.isd.esc4.net, 1002 San Jacinto St, La Porte (serves parts of southern Pasadena); Clear Creek Independent School District, www.ccisd.net, 2425 E Main St, League City, 281-284-0000 (serves parts of southern Pasadena); Goose Creek Independent Consolidated School District, www.gccisd.net, 4544 Interstate 10 E, Baytown, 281-420-4800 (serves Baytown)

Community Publications: *Pasadena Citizen*, www.thepasadenacitizen.com; *Baytown Sun*, www.baytownsun.com; *Deer Park Progress*, www.deerparkprogress.com

Community Resources: Transtar, www.houstontranstar.org; Pasadena Chamber of Commerce, www.pasadenachamber.org, 4334 Fairmont Pkwy, Pasadena, 281-487-7871; Baytown Chamber of Commerce, www.baytownchamber.com, Amegy Bank Bldg, 1300 Rollingbrook, Ste 400, Baytown, 281-422-8359; Deer Park Chamber of Commerce, www.deerpark.org, 110 Center St, Deer Park, 281-479-1559

Public Transportation: Lynchburg Ferry, 1001 S Lynchburg Rd, Baytown, 281-424-3521

NORTH HOUSTON SHIP CHANNEL AREA

The North Houston Ship Channel Area encompasses Channelview, North Shore, Galena Park, Jacinto City, and unincorporated parts of Sheldon. This is a heavily industrial area mixed with some suburban communities.

Channelview, an oil refinery town, is home to many of the refinery and factory workers that work at the local plants. Housing options here include mobile home communities, newly constructed and older single-family residential homes in a range of styles and sizes (two-story, new brick homes in typical suburban neighborhoods, large acreage in the country, and older small one-story homes with wood siding), and apartments.

North Shore is the newest community in the North Channel area, and most of the new home construction in the area is concentrated here. Smaller neighborhoods include **Cloverleaf, Hidden Forest, Home Owned Estates, New Forest, Pine Trails, River Grove, Riviera East,** and **Woodforest**. The references to woods and forests are a tribute to this quiet community's location among the tall pine trees of east Harris County.

HOUSTON: EAST OF HOUSTON

Galena Park began as a farming and ranching community called Clinton. After the opening of the Port of Houston, the town's character slowly evolved into today's heavily industrial city. At the turn of the 20th century its location along the Houston Ship Channel attracted oil companies that needed the warm shallow waters of the Gulf to transport their oil to other destinations. The town's name was later changed to Galena, after the oil company that built the first refinery here. Today, Galena Park is considered part of east Houston. Many of the homes here are small, plain, one-story houses with wood siding and range from $70,000 to $100,000. Other residents live in apartments spread throughout the area.

Jacinto City is named for its location near the San Jacinto battleground. It started in 1941 as a small subdivision built by Houston developer Frank Sharp. The initial residents were shipyard workers and employees from the local steel and war plants. Today most of the residents work at local petrochemical refineries. Jacinto City is a solidly Hispanic working to lower class community. The housing here is similar to nearby Galena Park—small one-story homes and apartments.

Websites: www.ci.jacinto-city.tx.us, www.galenaparktexas.com, www.houstontx.gov

Area Codes: 713, 281, 832

Zip Codes: 77530, 77547, 77029

Post Offices: Channelview Station, 531 Sheldon Rd, Channelview; Galena Park Station, 1805 Clinton Dr, Galena Park

Police Departments: Houston Police Department: East Freeway Storefront, 12001 E Fwy, Houston, 713-637-2120; Galena Park Police Department, 2207 Clinton Dr, Galena Park, 713-675-3471; Jacinto City Police Department, 10429 Market St, Jacinto City, 713-672-2455

Emergency Hospitals: Triumph Hospital East Houston, www.triumph-healthcare.com, 15101 E Fwy, Channelview, 832-200-5500; East Houston Regional Medical Center, www.easthoustonrmc.com, 13111 E Fwy, Houston, 713-393-2000

Libraries: Harris County Public Library, www.hcpl.net: Jacinto City Branch, 921 Akron St, 713-673-3237; Galena Park Branch, 1500 Keene St, Galena Park, 713-450-0982; North Channel Branch, 15741 Wallisville Rd, Houston, 281-457-1631

Adult Education: San Jacinto College, www.sjcd.cc.tx.us: Galena Park High School Extension Center, 1000 Keene St, Galena Park, 281-459-7103; Galena Park Community Resource/Training Center, 1721 16th St, Galena Park, 713-672-4606

Public Education: Channelview Independent School District, www.cvisd.org, 1403 Sheldon Rd, Channelview, 281-452-8002; Galena Park Independent School District, www.galenaparkisd.com, 14705 Woodforest Blvd, Houston, 832-386-1000 (Galena Park neighborhoods south of Market St, North Shore, and Jacinto City); Houston Independent School District, www.houstonisd.org, 4400 W 18th St, Houston, 713-556-6005 (Galena Park neighborhoods north of Market St)

Community Publications: *Houston Chronicle*, www.chron.com

Community Resource: North Channel Chamber of Commerce, www.northchannelarea.com, I-10 East, Ste 100, Houston, 713-450-3600

Public Transportation: Harris County Metropolitan Transit Authority, www.ridemetro.org: Maxey Park and Ride, *Bus:* 137, 236

LA PORTE AREA

As far back as the 1920s and 1930s, La Porte was well known as a seaside resort and recreational community. Popular big bands of the day, such as the Benny Goodman Orchestra, performed for visitors and summer residents at the Sylvan Beach Amusement Park in the nearby city of Shoreacres. After World War II, the growing petrochemical industry along the ship channel attracted new residents to the city. Though many of its residents still consider La Porte a small vacation village, it is also a residential community for employees of nearby refineries and industries along the ship channel. Nonetheless, many still visit for a nice weekend getaway. The town's main street features many unique shops and antique stores. More famously, it is home to the San Jacinto Monument, which commemorates Texas's independence, and the Battleship Texas, which served in World War I and II. Many Houstonians have boats or vacation homes in the La Porte/Bayshore area, including the nearby towns of Morgan's Point and Shoreacres. La Porte/Bayshore has apartments, townhomes, condominiums, and single-family residential homes that range from the relatively affordable to the very expensive. One-story homes located in neighborhoods or new planned communities occupy the more affordable end of the market. At the opposite end are million-dollar waterfront properties on large parcels of land. Of course, La Porte/Bayshore also offers everything else in between.

The **City of Morgan's Point,** a charming resort city, is historically significant as the origin of the Yellow Rose of Texas, which, legend has it, refers to a mulatto slave girl who warned the town of the approaching Mexican Army during the battle for Texas's independence. The founder, Colonel James Morgan, owner of the Morgan Plantation, did own a slave girl named Emily, who is reputed to be the basis for the Yellow Rose of Texas. This small town features expensive waterfront property, large two-story brick homes, and older one-story homes with wood siding.

The **City of Shoreacres** is home to the Houston Yacht Club and a bird sanctuary. This small bayside town is partly in Chambers and partly in Harris County. Some of the neighborhoods here tend to be heavily covered by trees, while others have no curbs or sidewalks. In addition to homes set in a typical neighborhood, you'll also find homes with waterfront views and on large acres surrounded by trees.

Websites: www.ci.la-porte.tx.us, www.cityofshoreacres.us, www.morganspoint-tx.com

Area Codes: 281, 409

Zip Code: 77571

Post Office: LaPorte Station, 801 W Fairmont Pkwy, La Porte

Police Departments: La Porte Police Department, 915 S 8th St, La Porte, 281-471-3811; Morgan's Point Police Department, 1415 E Main St, La Porte, 281-471-2171; Shoreacres Police Department, 601 Shoreacres Blvd, Shoreacres, 281-471-3340
Library: Harris County Public Library, www.hcpl.net: La Porte Branch, 600 S Broadway St, La Porte, 281-471-4022
Emergency Hospitals: Mainland Medical Center, www.mainlandmedical.com, 6801 Emmet F. Lowry Expy, Texas City, 409-938-5000; University of Texas Medical Branch Galveston, www.utmb.edu, 301 University Blvd, Galveston, 409-772-2618; San Jacinto Methodist Center, www.methodisthealth.com/sanjacinto, 4401 Garth Rd, Baytown, 281-420-8600; Bayshore Medical Center, www.bayshoremedical.com, 4000 Spencer Hwy, Pasadena, 713-359-2000
Public Education: La Porte Independent School District, www.laporte.isd.esc4.net, 1002 San Jacinto St, La Porte, 281-604-7000
Community Publication: Galveston County Daily News, www.galvestondailynews.com
Community Resources: Shoreacres City Hall, 601 Shoreacres Blvd, Shoreacres, 281-471-2244; Morgan's Point City Hall, 1415 E Main St, Morgan's Point; La Porte–Bayshore Chamber of Commerce, www.laportechamber.org, 712 W Fairmont Pkwy, La Porte, 281-471-1123
Public Transportation: none

BAY AREA

The Bay Area lies between Houston and Galveston and covers parts of Harris County, Chambers County, Brazoria County, and Galveston County. Originally centered around the fishing and agricultural industries, its economy has diversified since the 1930s to include the petrochemical, tourism, and aerospace industries. In the 1930s, oil was discovered in many of the communities here, which contributed to the temporary increase in the populations of many Bay Area communities. The population increased permanently and dramatically after 1961, when it was announced that NASA, which originally had offices in Houston, would be building its Mission Control (Johnson Space Center) here. Today, NASA and aerospace-related companies are the major employers in the Bay Area. It is probably more accurate to say that Houston is the Bayou City and the Bay Area is Space City.

In addition, the region's temperate climate draws visitors here year 'round. The water in this part of the Gulf of Mexico is mostly brown, which is its natural color. Heavy sediment and shallow waters produce a muddy-colored surface that resembles the waters of the Mississippi River. Though some people enjoy swimming in the warm Gulf waters, boating and fishing are by far the most popular activities. Neighborhoods and communities in the Bay Area include **Clear Lake, Clear Lake Shores, El Lago, League City, Kemah, Nassau Bay, Seabrook, South Shore Harbour, Taylor Lake Village, Victory Lakes,** and **Webster**.

Because of their proximity to the Gulf of Mexico, the communities in this area are vulnerable to hurricanes and strong tropical storms. After Hurricanes Katrina and Rita devastated much of the Gulf Coast in 2005, the Galveston-Houston area learned much about what it takes to evacuate millions of people from the path of a destructive storm. The most recent hurricane as of this publication, Hurricane Ike, was a mere Category 2 (out of 5 destruction levels) yet still took at least 195 lives and wiped out several coastal communities. Ike now is listed as the second costliest hurricane in the US. Residents choosing to live in the Bay area should be knowledgeable of and prepared for mandatory and voluntary evacuations. The Greater Houston Transportation and Emergency Center's website (Transtar), www.houstontranstar.org, provides a map with evacuation routes. Evacuation orders are given by each city's mayor, and by the county judge in unincorporated areas. Further information on hurricane preparedness can be found at the appropriate municipality's website. In addition, the Texas Governor's Office of Emergency Management has established a 211 hotline that those with special healthcare needs and individuals with no transportation can use to register *in advance* for transportation.

CLEAR LAKE

Even though Clear Lake is part of Houston, it certainly doesn't feel like it. Whereas the rest of Houston is an active urban environment with lush green vegetation and large concrete freeways snaking through it, Clear Lake is a laid-back seaside town. Instead of freeways or greenery, marinas with boats and yachts dot the landscape. You get the feeling that Clear Lake is a separate town. In fact, it once was. Unlike Houston, Clear Lake did not experience the same downturn in the housing market in the 1980s because it was largely unaffected by the oil bust. Its economic base is different and largely independent from Houston's. Clear Lake relies on the tourism and aerospace industries. NASA originally had offices in Houston, but when it decided to build a mission control center in 1961, it chose this area. As a result, owners of the nearby property decided to develop it for residential use. It's interesting to note that though NASA is often associated with Houston, it actually is located in Clear Lake City. Apparently Houston took notice of this also and decided that NASA, and thus Clear Lake, should be within Houston. Despite much protest from the residents, Houston annexed Clear Lake in 1977.

Clear Lake is named after the large lake next to it. The area is low lying, and there is a noticeable difference in the elevation between here and downtown Houston. This is generally an upper-middle-income area. Homes here include vacation homes, apartments, mansions, and single-family residential homes. The population here is diverse and highly educated. Many of them are engineers, most of whom work in the aerospace industry.

The Clear Lake area communities are:

- Spanish for "the lake," **El Lago** is located on Taylor Lake, Clear Lake, and NASA Parkway (also called NASA Road 1 and Farm Road 528). Pirate Jean Lafitte and his gang once hid out in what is now El Lago. The area is home to many aerospace employees and is very proud of the numerous astronauts who reside or previously resided here. Residents mostly live in apartments and single-family homes. There are also several condo complexes in El Lago, though some of them are owned as weekend vacation getaways. You'll also find a diverse selection of single-family homes, including million-dollar homes and large two-story brick homes.
- **Nassau Bay** homes are more affordable than those in Clear Lake and include a variety of options. Prospective residents can choose from lakeside estates, apartments, townhomes, single-family residential homes, and condominiums. It attracts many individuals employed in the aerospace and petrochemical industries. Nassau Bay is located on Nassau Lake across from FM 528.
- **Taylor Lake Village** is located on Taylor Lake, west of Seabrook. It is strictly a residential community, and no commercial businesses are allowed to establish here. This semi-exclusive community has some of the area's priciest homes that average in the $200,000 to $600,000 range. Some of the more expensive homes have waterfront views, boat houses, large yards, acreage, and other luxurious amenities.
- **Seabrook** is right on Galveston Bay and Clear Lake, next to the town of Kemah. It is a prime place to dock your boat or have a vacation home. Most of Seabrook is along the waterfront. The town is known for its fresh seafood markets, coastal bird sanctuary, antique stores, and shops featuring local artists. It has one of the largest populations in the Bay Area. Seabrook offers housing options for a range of income levels. There are apartments, townhomes, condominiums, and single-family residential homes. Many of the residences here have beautiful views of the waterfront. Homes range from middle-class suburban, two-story brick homes to older, smaller one-story homes. On the extreme end are million-dollar houses and mansions.
- **Webster** is on State Hwy 3 and the Galveston, Houston, and Henderson railroad 20 miles south of Houston and 3 miles west of the Lyndon B. Johnson Space Center. In 1879, James Webster, leader of a group of English settlers, settled it as Gardentown. In 1904, 70 Japanese farmers settled here to grow rice and oranges. In addition to single-family residences, there are also several established low-rise condominium complexes and townhomes here. Homes range from affordable single-story residences to two-story brick suburban-style homes, waterfront property, and homes on several acres.

Websites: www.houstontx.gov, www.nassaubay.com, www.ellago-tx.com, www.cityofwebster.com
Area Code: 281

Zip Codes: 77062, 77058, 77586, 77598

Post Offices: Albert Thomas Station, 14917 El Camino Real, Houston; Nassau Bay Station, 18214 Upper Bay Rd, Houston; Seabrook Station, 1600 2nd St, Seabrook; Webster Station, 17077 Texas Ave, Webster

Police Precincts and Departments: Houston Police Department: Clear Lake Substation, 2855 Bay Area Blvd, Houston, 281-218-3800; Nassau Bay Police Department, 1800 NASA Pkwy, Nassau Bay, 281-333-4200; El Lago Police Department, 98 Lakeshore Dr, Seabrook, 281-326-1098; Lakeview Police Department, 500 Kirby Rd, Seabrook, 281-326-5900 (Taylor Lake Village); Webster Police Department, www.websterpd.com, 217 Pennsylvania Ave, Webster, 281-332-2426

Emergency Hospitals: Clear Lake Regional Medical Center, www.clearlakermc.com, 500 Medical Center Blvd, Webster, 281-332-2511; Christus St. John Hospital, www.christusstjohn.org, 18300 St. John Dr, Nassau Bay, 281-333-5503

Libraries: Harris County Public Library, www.hcpl.net: Clear Lake City-County Freeman Branch, 16616 Diana Lane, Houston, 281-488-1906; Evelyn Meador Branch, 2400 Meyer Rd, Seabrook, 281-474-9142

Adult Education: University of Houston Clear Lake, www.uhcl.edu, 2700 Bay Area Blvd, Houston, 281-283-7600

Public Education: Clear Creek Independent School District, www.ccisd.net, 2425 E Main St, League City, 281-284-0000

Community Publications: *Houston Chronicle*, www.chron.com; *Bay Area Citizen*, www.yourhoustonnews.com/bay_area

Community Resources: City of Houston–Clear Lake, 2855 Bay Area Blvd, Houston, 281-218-3800; Taylor Lake Village City Hall, 500 Kirby Rd, Seabrook, 281-326-2843; Nassau Bay City Hall, 1800 NASA Pkwy, Houston, 281-333-2677; El Lago City Hall, 98 Lakeshore Dr, El Lago, 281-326-1951; Seabrook City Hall, 1700 1st St, Seabrook, 281-291-5600; Webster City Hall, 101 Pennsylvania St, Webster, 281-332-1826; Clear Lake Area Chamber of Commerce, www.clearlakearea.com, 1201 E NASA Pkwy, Houston, 281-488-7676

GALVESTON COUNTY

Galveston County has many small cities and towns that are popular tourist destinations and weekend getaways. The continually growing cruise industry in Galveston has brought more and more visitors to the city and surrounding areas. Some like it so much that they have purchased vacation or permanent homes on the isle. Living in this county has its rewards, but like Bay Area residents, those in Galveston County must be prepared to evacuate during hurricane season. The communities in this county are even more vulnerable to hurricanes than those in the Bay Area because little to nothing separates them from the Gulf of Mexico. City websites provide good hurricane preparation and evacuation tips. Many of them have local numbers to contact if special assistance is needed during evacuation. In addition, the Texas Governor's Office of Emergency Management has established a 211 hotline that those with special healthcare needs and individuals with no transportation can use to register *in advance* for transportation. Other resources include the local media and the Greater Houston Transportation and Emergency Center's website, www.houstontranstar.org, which provides a map with evacuation routes.

KEMAH

Minutes from Clear Lake, this charming seaside town is a favorite weekend getaway for Houstonians and residents of neighboring communities. Streets are lined with colorfully painted, quaint, one-story wood frame cottages that house local shops. Kemah's buildings are built close together, which makes it convenient to walk from place to place. Before the Kemah Boardwalk was built in the 1990s by well-known Houston restaurateur Tillman Fertitta, Kemah was a lovely and quiet place for a day trip. It still is, although more crowded and ostentatious. The Boardwalk was constructed to feature the dozen or so restaurants owned by Fertitta's Landry Corporation. Designed as a family-friendly entertainment/food complex, it has become a popular draw. The wooden boardwalk wraps around the waterfront, providing diners with a view of the Gulf of Mexico and an opportunity to soak in the breeze coming off the water. A giant Ferris wheel and other carnival rides and games are located on the boardwalk. The boardwalk offers a free way to have fun as it costs nothing to sit along it and enjoy the view. The other big draw here in Kemah is boating. The marina is packed with rows and rows of sailboats, motorboats, and yachts. The town was originally a shrimping village, and you can still see the shrimp boats coming in from the day's catch at dusk. In addition to the older quaint homes, newer and more ostentatious homes recently have been built in Kemah. Several of these are multimillion-dollar homes or mansions.

Clear Lake Shores, a small island community with approximately 1,200 residents, is also a vacation destination. Most of the homes in this community, surrounded by water on three sides and a mile from Galveston Bay, are on stilts. Clear Lake Shores is located on the southeastern side of Clear Lake at the entrance to Jarboe Bayou, where a water bird sanctuary and animal habitat are under development. The town has four major marinas and is home to several yacht clubs. Clear Lake Shores has a peaceful and quiet small-town atmosphere but is near the conveniences of Clear Lake City.

Website: www.kemah.net
Area Code: 281
Zip Code: 77565
Post Office: Kemah Station, 1129 Hwy 146, Kemah

Police Departments: Kemah Police Department, 1401 Hwy 146, Kemah, 281-334-5414; Clear Lake Shores Police Department, 1006 S Shore Dr, Kemah, 281-334-1034

Emergency Hospitals: Clear Lake Regional Medical Center, www.clearlakermc.com, 500 Medical Center Blvd, Webster, 281-332-2511; Christus St. John Hospital, www.christusstjohn.org, 18300 St. John Dr, Nassau Bay, 281-333-5503

Public Education: Clear Creek Independent School District, www.ccisd.net, 2425 E Main St, League City, 281-284-0000

Community Publications: *Bay Area Citizen,* www.yourhoustonnews.com/bay_area; *Galveston County Daily News,* www.galvestondailynews.com

Community Resources: Kemah City Hall, 603 Bradford Ave, Kemah, 281-334-3181; Clear Lake Shores City Hall, 1006 South Shore Dr, Clear Lake Shores, 281-334-2799; Clear Lake Area Chamber of Commerce, www.clearlakearea.com, 1201 E NASA Pkwy, Houston, 281-488-7676; Kemah Boardwalk, www.kemahboardwalk.com, Bradford and 2nd St, Kemah

LEAGUE CITY

League City is much like Clear Lake, a waterfront community whose residents largely work in the aerospace and tourism industries or nearby petrochemical refineries. Boating is a popular recreational activity here as well. Pockets of the town contain charming tree-lined commercial districts. League City has many waterfront homes, houses with views of the lake or bay, golf course communities, historic turn-of-the-century homes, and single-family residential neighborhoods. League City's location, character, and vacation-town feel lend to it a nice quality of life. It features several waterside resorts that are visited mostly by Houstonians. It is located on the south shore of Clear Lake and along I-45, which goes directly to Houston, 20 miles away.

One of the most notable areas here is **South Shore Harbour**, a master-planned community located along Clear Lake. Developers have attempted to re-create a resort-style atmosphere with palm trees and waterways. This community is ideal for those who like to live near the water. Many of the subdivisions, or villages as they are called here, have homes on the water where owners can dock their boats.

Another area to consider is **Victory Lakes**, a master-planned community that features seven lakes, walking trails, a golf course, and a recreational center. It is located directly on I-45 South at Highway 646.

Websites: www.leaguecity.com, southshoreharbour.com
Area Code: 281
Zip Code: 77573
Post Office: League City Station, 240 W Galveston St, League City
Police Department: League City Police Department, www.lcpd.com, 500 W Walker St, League City, 281-332-2566

Library: League City Helen Hall Library, http://leaguecity.com/index.aspx?NID=1277, 100 W Walker, League City, 281-554-1111

Emergency Hospitals: Clear Lake Regional Medical Center, www.clearlakermc.com, 500 Medical Center Blvd, Webster, 281-332-2511; Christus St. John Hospital, www.christusstjohn.org, 18300 St. John Dr, Nassau Bay, 281-333-5503

Public Education: Clear Creek Independent School District, www.ccisd.net, 2425 E Main St, League City, 281-284-0000

Community Publication: *Galveston County Daily News*, www.galvestondailynews.com

Community Resources: League City City Hall, 300 W Walker St, League City, 281-554-1000; Clear Lake Area Chamber of Commerce, www.clearlakearea.com, 1201 E NASA Pkwy, Houston, 281-488-7676

Public Transportation: Harris County Metropolitan Authority, www.ridemetro.org: Bay Area Park and Ride, *Bus:* 246

GALVESTON

This barrier island was the scene of the worst hurricane in US history. The unnamed hurricane of 1900 completely flattened what was at the time Texas's wealthiest town and changed the city forever. At the turn of the 20th century, Galveston was a bustling commercial center with the largest cotton port in the nation. In fact, it was referred to as the Wall Street of the South. The city displayed its wealth through its elegant and ornate buildings. Galveston was Texas' original "melting pot"—between 1846 and 1948, more than 130,000 immigrants made their way through the port. Those who remained in Galveston helped create a cosmopolitan and international flavor in this island city. Many of the historic Victorian buildings and mansions managed to survive the 1900 hurricane and now serve as tourist attractions. Today a 7-foot high seawall protects Galveston. The island, however,

Galveston

Galveston

never returned to its former glory after that early devastating hurricane. The city continued to play a secondary role to the emerging city of Houston, 50 miles away.

These days, Galveston is best known as a weekend getaway and relies heavily on the tourism industry. It is also home to world-class medical facilities connected to the University of Texas Medical Branch as well as ocean-oriented education via Texas A&M University at Galveston. Galveston was experiencing a resurgence in popularity, including a small cruise ship industry that developed around the Port of Galveston, when September 2008 brought Hurricane Ike to its shores. The resulting devastation from this "mere" Category 2 storm was most costly in terms of storm surge. Casualties on the island and nearby peninsulas numbered in the hundreds, and the storm is now listed as the second costliest in US history. Galveston all but shut its doors as hardy residents rebuilt. Since then, a full-on campaign to bring visitors back to the island has worked. The tourists are back, the hospitals reopened, and rebuilding continues. Moody Gardens, Schlitterbahn Water Park, and other attractions have all done their part to lure visitors onto the island. The risk of hurricanes has not deterred homebuyers, who are attracted by oceanfront views and seaside living. Homes closer to the water are built on stilts while homes farther inland are not. Galveston's restored Victorian residences, however, remain its showcase homes. Much of the new construction primarily has been high-rise condominiums near the coastline.

Incorporated areas on or near Galveston include the **Village of Tiki Island** (www.villageoftikiisland.com), **Jamaica Beach**, **High Island**, and **Crystal Beach**.

Website: www.cityofgalveston.org
Area Code: 409
Zip Codes: 77550, 77551, 77553, 77554
Post Offices: Galveston Station, 601 25th St, Galveston; Bob Lyons Station, 5826 Broadway St, Galveston

Police Department: Galveston Police Department, www.galvestonpd.com, 2517 Ball St, Galveston, 409-797-3702

Emergency Hospital: University of Texas Medical Branch Galveston, www.utmb.edu, 301 University Blvd, Galveston, 409-772-2618

Library: Galveston County Public Library System: Rosenberg Library, www.rosenberg-library.org, 2310 Sealy Ave, Galveston, 409-763-8854

Adult Education: University of Texas Medical Branch, www.utmb.edu, 301 University Blvd, Galveston, 409-772-2618; Texas A&M Galveston, www.tamug.edu, 200 Seawolf Pkwy, Galveston

Public Education: Galveston Independent School District, www.gisd.org, 3904 Ave T, Galveston, 409-766-5100

Community Publication: *Galveston County Daily News*, www.galvestondailynews.com

Community Resources: Galveston Historical Foundation, www.galvestonhistory.org; Galveston Convention and Entertainment, www.galveston.com; Galveston Chamber of Commerce, www.galvestonchamber.org, 519 25th St, Galveston, 409-763-5326

Public Transportation: Island Transit, www.islandtransit.net/main.htm

TEXAS CITY AND LA MARQUE

Texas City

Some of the nation's largest oil refineries are located in Texas City. Twice they've made national headlines when explosions at the docks in 1947 and in 2005 at the British Petroleum plant killed more than 600 people and injured hundreds more. Residents who live in the shadows of the neighboring petrochemical plants, often in small one-story wood frame homes, occasionally may be told to stay indoors or even evacuated when there is a chemical leak, fire, or explosion. Tall sirens dot the city's landscape, ready to blow in an emergency. Despite the danger, the city is proud of its history and shows it off at Bay Street Park with its Wings of Heritage Display. Texas City traces its history back to the days of the Republic of Texas in the 1830s, and some of the original buildings are still in use today. Farther away from the plants, residential neighborhoods tend to be bigger and newer. Anything from apartments to modest brick, one-story homes and large grand homes are available.

La Marque

La Marque was historically known as Highlands, a small farming community until the industrialization of the area. Its population grew as employees from the refineries and factories in nearby Texas City moved in. Several new subdivisions with affordable homes have been constructed in this primarily residential community. Many people come to La Marque to visit its bird sanctuary, the Gulf Greyhound

Park, and outlet shopping. Other smaller towns in the area include **Dickinson** (www.ci.dickinson.tx.us) and **Bacliff**.

Websites: www.texas-city-tx.org, www.ci.la-marque.tx.us
Area Code: 409
Zip Codes: 77590, 77591, 77568
Post Offices: Texas City Station, 2002 11th Ave N, Texas City; La Marque Station, 509 Laurel St, La Marque
Police Departments: Texas City Police Department, 1004 9th Ave N, Texas City, 409-643-5760; La Marque Police Department, 409-938-9269
Emergency Hospital: Mainland Medical Center, www.mainlandmedical.com, 6801 Emmet F. Lowry Expy, Texas City, 409-938-5000
Libraries: Moore Memorial Library (Texas City), 1701 9th Ave N, Texas City, 409-643-5979; La Marque Public Library, 1011 Bayou Rd, La Marque, 409-938-9270
Public Education: Texas City Independent School District, www.tcisd.org, 1041 Ninth Ave N, Texas City, 409-942-2713; La Marque Independent School District, http://66.60.230.134/education/components/scrapbook/, 1727 Bayou Rd, La Marque, 409-938-4251
Community Publication: *Galveston County Daily News*, www.galvnews.com
Community Resource: Texas City–LaMarque Chamber of Commerce, www.texas-citychamber.com, 8419 Emmett F Lowry Expy, Texas City, 409-935-1408

SOUTH OF HOUSTON

BRAZORIA COUNTY

Brazosport Area

Some of the lesser known gems of Brazoria County are clustered together in what's known as Brazosport. Most of the residential areas are small villages of beach houses that sit directly on the Gulf of Mexico beaches between Galveston and Matagorda bays.

The largest community in this region near the mouths of the Brazos and San Bernard rivers is **Lake Jackson**, a city with a population of a little more than 26,000 that was established in 1941 by the founders of Dow Chemical. Dow is still the area's major employer, but there are plenty more service-oriented employers, including small local businesses and large national chains. Driving through Lake Jackson is like stepping back in time to the 1950s. Mostly middle to upper-middle class, single-family neighborhoods are tidy and family-oriented, while zoning laws restrict businesses to a central location. Though it grows at a slow pace (just less than 2 percent from 2000 to 2010), Lake Jackson is now home to large medical centers and a thriving two-year school of higher learning, Brazosport College.

Lake Jackson

As it's a one-hour drive down Highway 288 from downtown Houston, some residents commute to and from Houston's Texas Medical Center, but for the most part Lake Jackson is in no hurry to boom like its closer-in neighbors, Pearland and Friendswood.

Clute adjoins Lake Jackson, but has a more working-class air about it. You'll find more multifamily dwellings here, along with trailer parks and warehouse businesses.

Websites: www.brazosport.org, www.lakejackson-tx.gov/pages, www.ci.clute.tx.us/pages/index.php

Pearland

This town's history dates back to the 1880s. Named for the abundance of pear trees in the area, Pearland grew fruit and figs as a cash crop. The devastating hurricane of 1900 destroyed most of the crops, but the community replanted and continued to produce fruit. As late as the 1960s, Pearland was a small agricultural community with fewer than 1,500 residents. Pearland has grown tremendously in the last decade, currently numbering over 91,000 residents. Largely a rural community, it has become one of the hottest suburban communities in Houston. Its selection of affordable housing and quiet atmosphere has attracted many homebuyers. Located partially within Harris, Brazoria, and Fort Bend counties, Pearland is directly south of downtown Houston, hence its popularity with medical professionals employed at the Texas Medical Center; State Highway 288 provides direct access. Pearland is also popular with downtown Houston workers because of the same easy travel route.

Two of the most notable master-planned communities here are Shadow Creek Ranch and Silverlake, both lake-themed communities. **Shadow Creek Ranch** homes range from the $140,000s to more than $1 million. **Silverlake's** homes are in similar varying price ranges. The construction of new subdivisions and ensuing commercial development has gradually transformed Pearland into a more suburban/urban environment, but the older neighborhoods are still rural in character, generally on narrow, curb-free roads densely covered by big oak trees. Farm property and country lots are still available in Pearland.

Friendswood

The Society of Friends, commonly known as Quakers, settled Friendswood in 1895. From its founding until the 1930s, it remained largely an agricultural Quaker community. When the Johnson Space Center was constructed 10 miles away in the 1960s, more people began to move here either to work for NASA or to commute to Houston. Since then, it has remained one of the area's major bedroom communities. Today, Friendswood is home to people of varying faiths and reflects the diversity of suburban Houston.

Websites: ci.pearland.tx.us, www.ci.friendswood.tx.us, silverlaketexas.com, shadowcreekranch.net
Area Codes: 281, 832
Zip Codes: 77581, 77584, 77546
Post Offices: Pearland Station, 3519 E Walnut St, Pearland; Friendswood Station, 310 Morningside Dr, Friendswood
Police Departments: Pearland Police Department, 2703 Veterans Dr, Pearland, 281-652-1100; Friendswood Police Department, 109 E Willowick Ave, Friendswood, 281-996-3318
Emergency Hospitals: Memorial Hermann Southeast Hospital, www.memorialhermann.org, 11800 Astoria Blvd, Houston, 281-929-6100; Christus St. John Hospital, www.christusstjohn.org, 18300 St. John Dr, Houston, 281-333-5503; Clear Lake Regional Medical Center, www.clearlakemc.com, 500 Medical Center Blvd, Webster, 281-332-2511
Libraries: Brazoria County Public Library System, www.bcls.lib.tx.us, 3522 Liberty Dr, 281-485-4876; Friendswood Public Library, www.friendswood.lib.tx.us, 416 S Friendswood Dr, Friendswood, 281-482-7135
Adult Education: Alvin Community College–Pearland College Center, ww2.alvincollege.edu, 2319 N Grand Blvd, Pearland, 281-756-3900
Public Education: Pearland Independent School District, www.pearlandisd.org, 2337 N Galveston Ave, Pearland, 281-485-3203; Alvin Independent School District, www.alvinisd.net, 301 E House St, Alvin, 281-388-1130 (portions of Pearland, including Shadow Creek Ranch subdivision); Friendswood Independent School District, www.friendswood.isd.tenet.edu, 108 E Shadowbend Ave, Friendswood, 281-482-1198

Community Publications: *Pearland Journal*, yourhoustonnews.com/pearland; *Friendswood Journal*, www.yourhoustonnews.com/friendswood

Community Resources: Pearland Chamber of Commerce, www.pearlandchamber.com, 3501 Liberty Dr, Pearland, 281-485-3634; Friendswood Chamber of Commerce, www.friendswood-chamber.com, 1100 S Friendswood Dr, Friendswood, 281-482-3329

INDEX

A

Addicks 35, 38, 39
Addicks/Barker 35, 38, 39
Afton Oaks 26
Airport 1, 42, 59, 68, 70, 73, 74
Aldine 68-70
Alief 32, 44-48
Allen Parkway 6
Astrodome/Reliant Center 24
Atascocita 74, 75
Audubon 18
Avalon 26, 54
Avalon Place 26
Avondale 18
Ayrshire 25

B

Bacliff 90
Bay Area 81, 83, 84, 86, 87
Bayou City 1, 81
Bayshore 77, 80, 81
Baytown 75, 77, 78, 81
Bear Creek 39
Bear Creek Park 39, 66
Bellaire 2, 19, 20, 22, 23, 40
Boulevard Oaks 24
Braeburn 44
Braes Heights 25
Braes Manor 25
Braes Oaks 25
Braes Terrace 25
Braeswood Place 25
Brays Bayou 15, 19, 22, 25, 40, 44

Brazosport 90
Brazos River 56, 57
Briar Court 31
Briar Forest 35
Briargrove 29, 30
Briar Grove Park 31
Buffalo Bayou 1, 6, 8, 9, 15, 26, 32-34
Bunker Hill Village 33, 34

C

Camp Logan 2, 10, 11, 32
Candlelight 59, 60, 61
Candlelight Estates/Oaks/Forest/Place/
   Plaza/Woods 60
Castle Court 18
Champion Forest 63, 66
Champions 68
Channelview 78, 79
Cherryhurst 18, 19
Cinco Ranch 37, 38
CityView 68
Clear Lake 81-87, 92
Cloverleaf 78
Clute 91
Copperfield 64, 66
Country Club Place 15
Courtlandt Place 18
Crestwood 2, 10, 12, 32
Cypress 1, 59, 61, 62, 63, 65, 66, 70
Cypress Creek Parkway 59, 63

D

Deer Park 75-78

Dickinson 90
Downtown 1, 3, 7, 10, 16

E

East Glenshire 43
East Houston 8, 9, 14, 15, 79
Eastwood 16
El Lago 83
Energy Corridor 35, 37

F

Fairfield 65, 66
Fifth Ward 9, 17
First Colony 53, 54
First Ward 8, 9
Flooding 25, 40, 41, 75
Fondren Southwest 42, 44
Fort Bend County 38, 46, 48, 49, 52, 54, 56, 57, 58
Fourth Ward 7-9
Friendswood 64, 65, 73, 91-93
Friendswood Development Company 65, 73

G

Galena Park 78, 79
Galleria 1, 10, 20, 28-30, 41
Galveston 87-89
Galveston Bay 77, 83, 85
Galveston County 81, 84, 86, 87, 89, 90
Garden Oaks 59-61
Gleannloch Farms 63, 66
Glen Brook 15
Glenshire 42, 43
Golfcrest 17
Grand Lakes 37
Greater Houston Transportation and Emergency Center 75, 82, 85
Greatwood 54
Greens Bayou 68
Greenspoint 63, 67-69, 74
Greenway Plaza 26-28, 74
Gulfgate 16, 17
Gulf of Mexico 81, 82, 84, 85, 90

H

Harrisburg 2, 16, 17

Harris County 10, 12, 14, 17, 19, 22, 23, 26, 28, 31, 32, 36, 38, 39, 41, 43, 48, 54, 55, 61, 65-70, 72, 75, 77-81, 84, 87
Harwin 44
Hedwig Village 33, 34, 36
Heights 12, 14
Hidden Forest 78
Highland Village 26, 27
Hillshire Village 33-35
Home Owned Estates 78
Houston Ship Channel 76, 78, 79
Humble 7, 36, 67, 73-75, 77
Hunters Creek 33, 34
Hurricanes 2, 39, 75, 82, 84, 87, 88, 91
Hyde Park 18

I

Idylwood 15
Imperial Valley 68
Inner Loop 2, 28, 32, 40, 44, 68
Inwood Forest 59

J

Jacinto City 78, 79
Jarboe Bayou 85
Jersey Village 62, 65
Johnson Space Center 81, 83, 92

K

Katy Area 36-39
Katy, City of 36, 37
Katy, Old Town 36
Kemah 81, 83, 85, 86
King Ranch 74
Kingwood 73-75
Klein 62, 63, 65, 66, 70

L

Lake Houston 73-75
Lake Jackson 90, 91
Lake Olympia 55
Lakeside Country Club 31
Lakeside Estates 31
La Marque 89, 90
Lancaster Place 18
La Porte 78, 80, 81
League City 78, 81, 84, 86, 87
Lindale Park 15
Linkwood 25, 40

INDEX

Little Oak Bayou 9
Lynchburg Ferry 77, 78

M

Magnolia 15-17, 67
Magnolia Park 15, 17
Manchester 17
Mason Park 15
Meadows Place 49, 52, 53
Medical Center 24
Memorial 32, 33
Memorial Area 32
Memorial Park 6, 10-12, 32, 36
Memorial Parkway 37
Memorial Villages 33, 34, 36
Memorial West 35
Meyerland 40, 41
Midtown 1-3, 7-10, 18
Mission Bend 35, 47
Missouri City 48, 52, 54-57
Montgomery County 66, 67, 70-73
Montrose 2, 6, 7, 16, 18, 19, 23, 28
Morgan's Point 80, 81
Museum District 1, 2, 18, 23, 26

N

NASA 1, 81-84, 86, 87, 92
NASA Parkway 83
Nassau Bay 81, 83, 84, 86, 87
Neartown 18, 19, 28
New Forest 78
New Territory 54
Norhill 13
Northeast Houston 73
North Houston Ship Channel Area 78
Northline 67
North Shore 78, 79
Northwest Houston 58
Nottingham Country 37

O

Oak Estates 26
Oak Forest 59-61
Old Braeswood 19, 22, 25
Old Town Katy 36
Old Town Spring 69
Outer Loop 28
Oyster Creek 55

P

Pasadena 75-78, 81
Pearland 91-93
Pecan Grove Plantation 57
Pecan Park 15
Pine Trails 78
Piney Point 33, 34

Q

Quail Valley 55

R

Reliant Stadium 20, 24, 41
Rice Military 2, 10, 11, 32
Rice University Area 23
Rice Village 21
Richmond 18, 19, 26, 29, 32, 39, 49, 56-58
Rivercrest 31
River Grove 78
River Oaks 1, 2, 12, 16, 18, 19, 26, 28, 29
Riverside Terrace 16
Riviera East 78
Roseland Estates 18
Rosenberg 57, 58, 89
Royal Palms 31
Royden Oaks 26

S

Sam Houston Tollway 31, 34, 59, 69
Sandlewood 33
Seabrook 81, 83, 84
Second Ward 8, 15
Settlers Way/Settlers Park/Settlers Grove 54
Shadow Creek Ranch 91, 92
Sharpstown 44-48
Sheldon 78, 79
Shenandoah 72
Shepherd Park 60
Shoreacres 80, 81
Sienna Plantation 55, 56
Silverlake 91, 92
Sixth Ward 9
Southampton 24
Southern Oaks 25
Southgate 24
South Loop Area 24
South Shore Harbour 81, 86
Southside Place 2, 7, 19, 21-23
Southwest Houston 39-41, 43, 48

Southwest Suburbs 48
Spring 33-36, 62, 65, 66, 69, 70-73
Spring Branch 34-36
Spring Branch Bayou 34, 35
Spring Valley 33-36
Stafford 49, 52, 53
Stella Link 25, 26, 40, 41
Sugar Creek 54
Sugar Land 46, 48, 52-54, 57, 58, 77
Sunset Heights 13

T

Tanglewood 29, 30
Taylor Lake 81, 83, 84
Teal Wood 33
Texas City 81, 89, 90
Texas Medical Center 2, 7, 10, 12, 18, 19, 22, 23, 25, 26, 28, 31, 41, 43, 91
Texas Southern University 9, 15, 16, 17
The Woodlands 63, 70-73
Third Ward 8, 9, 17
Timbergrove West 13
Tin Hall 61
Tomball 62, 65-67
Tour 18 74
Transtar 75, 78, 82

U

University Oaks 16
University of Houston 8-10, 15-17, 19, 38, 54, 84
Upper Kirby 2, 26, 27
Uptown 1, 28-30, 41

V

Victory Lakes 81, 86
Villages of Glenshire 43
Villages, The 33
Village West 31

W

Walnut Bend 31
Wards, The 8
Warrenton 33
Washington Corridor 11
Washington Terrace 16
Webster 81, 83, 84, 86, 87, 92
Westbury 41-43
Westchase 29, 31, 32

West End 10, 11, 20
West Glenshire 43
Westpark Tollway 47
West University Place 19-23
Westwood 44, 48
Whispering Oaks 33
White Oak Bayou 13, 60
Williams Tower 29
Willowbrook Mall 63
Winlow Place 18
Woodforest 78, 79
Woodlake/Woodlake Square 33
Woodland Heights 8, 13
Woodlands, The 63, 70-73

READER RESPONSE

WE WOULD APPRECIATE YOUR COMMENTS REGARDING THIS EDITION of the *Newcomer's Handbook® Neighborhood Guide for Houston*. If you've found any mistakes or omissions or if you would just like to express your opinion about the guide, please let us know. We will consider any suggestions for possible inclusion in our next edition, and if we use your comments, we'll send you a free copy of the new edition. Please e-mail us at readerresponse@firstbooks.com, or mail or fax this response form to:

Reader Response Department
First Books
6750 SW Franklin, Suite A
Portland, OR 97223-2542
Fax: 503.968.6779

Comments: _____

_____

_____

_____

_____

_____

_____

_____

_____

_____

Name: _____

Address: _____

_____

_____

Telephone: (   ) _____

Email: _____

6750 SW Franklin, Suite A
Portland, OR 97223-2542
P: 503.968.6777
www.firstbooks.com

FIRST BOOKS

RELOCATION RESOURCES

Utilizing an innovative grid and "static" reusable adhesive sticker format, **Furniture Placement and Room Planning Guide…Moving Made Easy** provides a functional and practical solution to all your space planning and furniture placement needs.

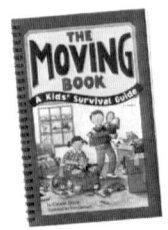

MOVING WITH KIDS?

Look into **The Moving Book: A Kids' Survival Guide**.

Divided into three sections (before, during, and after the move), it's a handbook, a journal, and a scrapbook all in one. Includes address book, colorful change-of-address cards, and a useful section for parents.

Children's Book of the Month Club "Featured Selection"; American Bookseller's "Pick of the List"; Winner of the Family Channel's "Seal of Quality" Award

And for your younger children, ease their transition with our brand-new title just for them, **Max's Moving Adventure: A Coloring Book for Kids on the Move**. A complete story book featuring activities as well as pictures that children can color; designed to help children cope with the stresses of small or large moves.

NEWCOMERSWEB.COM

Based on the award-winning *Newcomer's Handbooks*, **NewcomersWeb.com** offers the highest quality neighborhood and community information in a one-of-a-kind searchable online database. The following areas are covered: Atlanta, Austin, Boston, Chicago, Dallas–Fort Worth, Houston, Los Angeles, Minneapolis–St. Paul, New York City, Portland (Oregon), San Francisco, Seattle, Washington DC, and the USA.

NEWCOMER'S HANDBOOKS®

Regularly revised and updated, these popular guides are now available for Atlanta, Boston, Chicago, China, London, Los Angeles, Minneapolis–St. Paul, New York City, Portland, San Francisco Bay Area, Seattle, and Washington DC.

"Invaluable …highly recommended" – *Library Journal*

If you're coming from another country, don't miss the **Newcomer's Handbook® for Moving to and Living in the USA** by Mike Livingston, termed "a fascinating book for newcomers and residents alike" by the *Chicago Tribune*.

6750 SW Franklin Street
Portland, Oregon 97223-2542
Phone 503.968.6777 • Fax 503.968.6779
www.firstbooks.com

Printed by BoD in Norderstedt, Germany